# THE
# Trout
## AND THE Fly

# THE
# Trout
# AND THE Fly

## RAY OVINGTON

Illustrations by the Author

HAWTHORN BOOKS, INC.
*Publishers* / NEW YORK
A Howard & Wyndham Company

Chapters 1 and 2, "Trout Taketh Understanding" and "Drama of the Evening Rise," are based on articles in *Field & Stream*. What the Hell Is a Fly Rod?, a section of "Some Shorts on Tackle," chapter 5, was previously published by the *Fly Fisherman Magazine*.

THE TROUT AND THE FLY

Library of Congress Catalog Card Number: 76-24229
ISBN: 0-8015-7983-X
2 3 4 5 6 7 8 9 10

To the late Mark Kerridge—
a grand person, a perfectionist angler,
a fighter for stream conservation, a
lover of good fishing books and
dry martinis

# Contents

# THE Trout AND THE Fly

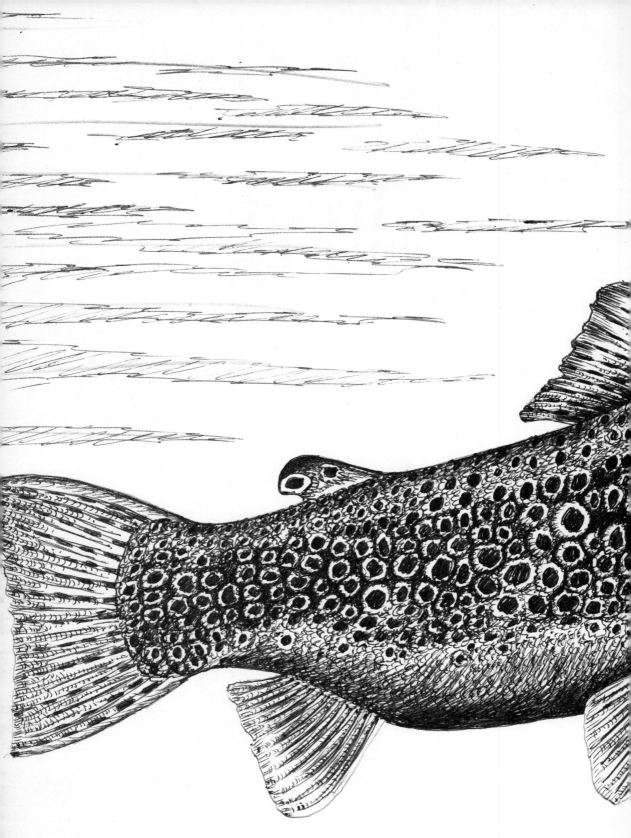

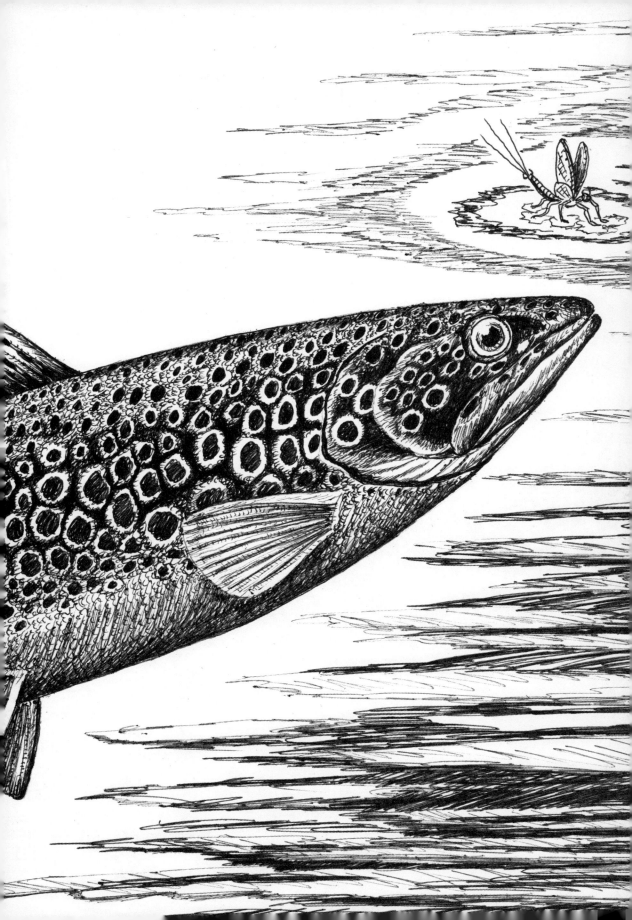

# Introduction

This book is a fifty-odd-year-old's version of his beliefs, theories, and the resultant conclusions gleaned from much practice in the art of fly fishing for trout. You will find much controversy here and perhaps some new angles on the sport of fly fishing, the tricks of tying unusual flies, and where to go.

If you are already a fly angler, you'll have developed many of your own opinions and deductions which might correspond to mine, or they may disagree violently. At my age and with a full lifetime of fishing behind me, I admit I'm opinionated and perhaps a bit adamant regarding the relative merits of a lot of fly-fishing theory and trouting lore that have come down the pike since Halford.

I've taken some nice trout from the brooks of New Brunswick and the Allagash in Maine, to the beautiful waters of Tennessee, New York, Pennsylvania, and New England. Those trout sharpened my rod hand. Michigan and Ontario—what memories! Then the big West—a trout angler's heaven—clear from British Columbia to Southern California and from Idaho and Montana to Mexico. The extremes of Newfoundland and Argentina blew my trouting mind. They all taught me something and much of it is here in these pages where I've tried to bring some semblance of simplicity to technique.

# 1
# Trout Taketh Understanding

It has been said that to catch a wily trout you have to be one. The next best thing is to explore the trout's domain in any way possible and to constantly train your eyes and senses in order to catch the trout in his act as he goes about the simple business of eating a living. I have done this for many years, stopping at nothing to gain an insight into the mysteries of the current.

Usually, the trout fisherman can see only a very few of the trout's activities, mainly the ones that are visible on the surface from where he is fishing. If the light is right and all conditions concur, the angler can see some of what's going on. But even the plain-sight surface splashes can be misinterpreted. Splashing water *can* look as if the trout is taking an insect from the surface, when in reality, his tail might be causing it, his head being pointed down, straight down. Naturally, in this pose and action, the trout would not likely show an interest in a floating fly. The angler, then, rightly concludes that he would be better off with wet flies, nymphs, or even a bucktail—anything but a dry fly, unless he wants to disregard this tip-off and play the way-out odds.

When trout are bottom feeding on nymphs, it is usually

in a rocky bottom section of a medium-fast stretch of water, perhaps near the end of a pool before the water shallows and splits into individual watercourses. This can also happen along the quieter edges of main currents, quieter water sections near the heads of big pools, and away from the actual drop-offs from shelving riffles. Here are found the various species of caddis fly larvae and a grand assortment of the several species of mayfly and stone-fly nymphs that abound in this type of water and on this kind of bottom.

Usually, the springtime finds the trout feeding almost exclusively on the bottom and in this fashion, since not too many hatches of insects have attracted their attention to the top of the water. The trout will be dislodging the nymphs and caddis fly larvae that are still living in their cases, some swinging in the current, all easily spotted by the trout. Since these "bugs" abound in great clusters, the trout congregate in such areas, picking off the insects at will, slithering along the rocks to uproot them, or in some cases, nosing along in a permanent "mudding," nose-down position.

This action can be seen plainly when the light is right. It is not limited to the early season. Quite often in mid-summer, in the period of hatches, trout will feed in this manner even when a hatch is in progress and will only give it up when enough of the passing nymphs and hatching insects distract their attention from the bottom. The obvious lure is the wet fly or nymph fished deep—actually bumped right along the bottom.

Tailing is a variation of bottom feeding except that it occurs in shallow water, either aside from the main current near the top of the pool or in the deep feeding lanes that string out near the waste-water sections at the tails of pools. Numbers of fish will be seen, and the usual deduction would be that a rise was taking place to surface insects. Only a close look will divulge the tails of the trout, not the snouts. A dry fly used here would be, of course, a farfetched bit of nonsense, for the attention of the fish is obviously down, not up.

Tailing is done at all times of the day and all season long when the light is not too bright over the water, for, remember, these shallow areas are generally well exposed. Similar to the deep-water bottom mudding, it is done when there are no hatches in evidence. They will return to it long after a hatch has passed on. Still hungry, they return to their "gardening."

Rainbow and brook trout tend to feed in this manner much more so than brown trout, since they are not prone to lie in the open current or stay in relatively exposed areas during the bright time of the day.

Freshly planted hatchery fish quickly take to this manner of feeding. I've seen such trout in a stream already bottom feeding, and it is usually quite a hatch that will cause them to rise to the surface. Maybe the hatchery personnel should train the trout by giving them floating pellets rather than the sinking kind!

When you catch a trout, no matter on what type of fly, inspect it for gravel and bits of leaves in the gullet. If it is full of such material, you have evidence of this type of feeding.

The alert angler can see the nymphs drifting perhaps a few inches below the surface of the water preparatory to hatching. When they are seen doing this near the surface, you can be certain of a good hatch coming on within a few minutes. Flashing will be seen in the fast water as the trout pick the nymphs off before they reach the surface film where they begin to disrobe. As the nymphs begin to actually cast their nymphal shuck in the surface film, the trout will be "nymphing" for them and will break the water surface with their tails or in a follow-through motion by taking the nymphs as they lunge upward from below. Many trout will be seen in this follow-through actually jumping into the air. A close look at them will show, as have my fast-action photos, that they had their mouths closed and that there was no insect ahead of them on the surface to jump down upon.

This all-important surface-film activity is where the wet fly, skittered or manipulated in an escaping-form-of-life technique of short jerks, is the method to employ. Look closely during the next few minutes and you'll see the substage, or dun stage, of the mayfly actually taking to the air, freed from its shuck. In the case of flies such as the Quill Gordon or March Brown, this change takes a longer time, and the insect struggles both with the film and the shedding process. A wet fly fished very light on top or a sunken type of soft-hackled dry fly is recommended.

7

Finally, when enough of the duns are floating on the surface, it is time to shift to the dry fly.

To really get the feel of this situation, allow one of the drifting nymphs to lodge in your hand in a bit of water. Chances are it will perform the change right before your eyes and fly away to shore. Now, you are really bearing witness. Again, inspect the innards of the trout and you find they were recently feeding on nymphs, some of their cases already cracked open.

There are three types of rises to the emerging dun: leaping from above, dimpling the water by coming straight from beneath, and a subsurface attack on a dun that causes the dorsal fin to disturb the surface. They are all typical in their approach. It is an impressive sight, especially when the action is unexpected. A single dun can be hatching above your position. Or a rise can be to any one of a dozen flies about to hatch in the feeding lane, working, as they will, right in and around your artificial. Note that they are freely turned by the current, whereas your imitation is not, so here it is wise to use the finest leader practical to give the fly freedom of movement. Keep a sharp eye out when the trout glides near. Hold back on your trigger finger when you see a trout break the water nearby. Nine times out of ten, if your line is tight, your strike will be too early and you'll claim that the trout are only making light hits. Actually, you pulled the fly away from the fish.

When you see the naturals close together, place your artificial in among them—one of a slightly smaller size and the same general color and shape. Control the drag, for this is important here, or keep it to an absolute minimum.

The brown trout may perform a characteristic airborne leap, as this species is prone to aerial acrobatics. Note that even in this type of rise he will be headed down to feed on the dun. Of course, brookies and rainbows will do this but not so generally. Browns usually rush the fly and brooks merely roll up under it like a shark taking a surface bait.

During the middle and late times of the season, usually at twilight during the dun hatch, the evening rise is the most dramatic in this respect. A pool, which half an hour before looked entirely devoid of fish, suddenly becomes crowded with action. Big trout seem to come from nowhere, and one wonders how it is possible for the pool to hold so many that have gone completely unnoticed during the foregoing hours.

A rise to an emerged dun is the most conventional of all the rise types and the easiest to identify. Other kinds of splashes may be confused with it, but sharp eyes can detect the actual taking of the dun from the surface when conditions are right. Usually, it is more obvious below the actual location of the hatch, since the transition from the taking of the emerging duns and those that have emerged can be quite confusing. Below the area of the hatch, when there are quite a number of duns sailboating the pool, the rise to the individual floating insects can easily be spotted.

The typical rise of the rainbow can be and is performed by all three species, but the rainbow is the more impressive performer. The type of rise is naturally dictated by the conditions around it. If the water is fast, the chances are that the trout will rush into the foam to the fly. When the surface is calmer, he can and does come up and over.

Then is the time for the dun patterns. The dry-fly technique, with all its subtleties of cast directions, is in order. When the trout are feeding on emerged duns, it is best to keep drag to a minimum, since the fly is not actually peforming any movement other than walking slightly on the surface, not fluttering or struggling as in the hatching sequence.

As to the pattern selection, I've found that a pattern slightly smaller and, on a clear day, lighter (on a dark day, darker) is the general idea to follow. During the dusk-time hatches, a darker fly is usually recommended, although this is hard to follow in such bad light. A white-winged pattern or a bivisible is then used.

The biggest trick to hooking fish that are rising to the emerged dun is in making sure you do not strike too fast. Often the quick response pulls the fly away, particularly during the fish's aerial rise.

The evening rise is one that can literally drive the dry-fly addict crazy. It is the rise to the adult or spinner stage of

the mayfly. Actually, three things are going on here. The adult flies, having cast their dun skins in the nearby bushes or trees or on the rocks, are now returning to the stream to find a mate. In the early season this flight comes before sunset, when what little warmth there was has dissipated. In the latter season the flight occurs at twilight, and in midsummer it usually starts just at dusk. Some of the insects are blown down to the surface, some light for an instant only to take off again.

The adult fly has little or no food value, since its energy is now all spent on producing eggs. The trout know this and are really after the eggs of the female. She dips down to the water in a tantalizing dance that is the continuation of the mating up-and-down zigzag, not unlike the ballet dancer performing her light, bouncing movements. When the insect touches the water ever so gently, the eggs drop off into the water, quickly descend, and attach themselves to the bottom stream rocks. The trout like those eggs.

There is hardly a fly-fisherman alive who has not wondered why trout will sometimes bump the knots of even the thinnest leader. Those knots look to the trout just like the egg sac clusters the mayflies are depositing. If you don't believe this, take a 7X tippet and tie on three short tippets. On the ends tie a size 20 or 22 hook with a small bit of yellow or gray yarn wound sparsely. You'll take trout!

With insects and hatches overlapping in the middle of the season, some will be hatching at the very time the spinners are performing their return flights. It is interesting to watch the trout turn from one to the other. If you are fishing a spinner and see the trout taking the duns, try that pattern. If the trout become selective to spinners, switch to a spider or lightly tied spinner imitation. It's a tricky business, and one that requires you to "see" before you can "do."

Despite the extreme activity of the life of a trout, he seems to find time to rest. Contrary to some authorities, he is not always on the feed. During the summer months when the water is low, clear, and warm, and the sun bright and dazzling, he prefers to sit out the midday shine in the comforting shade of a ledge rock and await the coolness of the evening before venturing out. Many times I have waded by "sleeping" trout and, despite trodding almost

upon them, have actually prodded them with the rod tip to dislodge them from their hold.

You'll find them almost asleep, since there are no insects hatching and no minnows moving nearby. Even a sparrow flying overhead will not cause them to move a fin.

If you were to inspect carefully all the bigger stones and rocks of the average run, particularly in the medium-shallow stretches down from the heads of pools, along the edges of main currents, and in the holes at the pool tails, you'd find many such fish hiding. Only a general overall glance at the pool would bring on the impression that there was not a fish in it. Those are the ones that make the place look like a crowded dance hall on Saturday night once the air has cooled the water and the lights are low.

How to catch this fellow? Personally, I wouldn't bother him, not now, at least. Let him rest until sundown. There are fast runs and eddies where the trout are bound to be more active. Oh, sure, just for target practice and for kicks, float a few flies over him to possibly entice him into striking. This *can* be done if you have the patience to throw a fly, maybe twenty times, and drift it right over him, draging free with an expert delivery each time. He won't bolt if you goof, but since he's not hungry, he'll just let you practice while he snoozes.

A dimpling swat at drifting flies is a touchy type of rise. The fish are just hanging there in the current with their snouts hardly breaking the surface film. They are merely waiting for the insects to drift by and tickle their noses. This is the midge-feeding position. It is seen over a deep hole where the water surface is ruffled and so offers some protection from the penetrating sunlight. It also happens at twilight or where the forest shades that particular part of the stream. Note that the snouts will almost be breaking the surface. The trout are not rising to any specific insect and may hang there indefinitely, changing positions occasionally as the current itself moves them about. They'll gently wave their tails, but you'll see that they keep returning to the actual feed lane where the insects will be drifting by. They won't waste time out of the path of circulation.

Trout that normally will not put up with fish their size in the lairs on the bottom will feed in the open almost side by side, rarely chasing each other away. This is a very difficult pose to cast a fly to, since the least line or leader disturbance will send the whole lot of fish scampering back to their homes behind rocks or into the deepest parts of the pool. When the fish do open their mouths, it is ever so slightly and appears as a mere ripple, hardly discernible if the water surface is at all churned up or flexed by the current or breeze. Seen from a distance against reflection and glare, one would swear that it was only a tiny chub or minnow performing, but it could be a trout of magnificent proportions if one were in the right position to see the real thing.

This peculiarity of the trout is also a part of the picture when they are feeding on drifting blackfly and midge larvae. These insects drift in the surface film by the thousands, and it is the trout's habit to merely nose into them and feel the insects with its lips and open its jaws for the flies to be sucked in. Quite often a big old brown will be seen cruising along with his snout making a very slight wake on the surface. This is detected on lakes when the water is glassy. A close look shows him with his mouth cracked open just a bit most, if not all, of the time. To present a tiny size 20 to him under these conditions is quite an art, and it's effective if you can pull it off.

A trout on the alert is the pose that most anglers hardly ever see. He is usually well hidden, perhaps between rocks and submerged branches. At least he will be in a position where any insects floating with the current will flow by him and become tangled in the branches of the snag or be swayed out to him by the current as it slips by the rocks.

He's there because that is his domain. No other trout will be too close. He may have to fight for the position, or he has taken it up after some lucky angler caught his predecessor. Every fin is poised for quick reaction if a succulent insect comes near or if a minnow ventures too close.

He's a sucker for your flies, no matter what pattern or style, just as long as your delivery doesn't scare him down deep and out of circulation. If you do frighten him, you'll not be the wiser. You'll merely conclude that there was no trout there or, if there was, he simply wasn't interested. Walk along the bank of any trout stream where there are overhangs or underwater rocks that jut out. You'll see trout there that you never realized lived in the stream. Again, this is taking time out from casting, but the evidence in this case will pay off once you are on the water.

You'll automatically assume that there are fish waiting to be caught in these places. If you have any doubts and want to see first and fish later, you can go ashore, peer down, and your evidence will be yours alone.

A fish in this position is rarely selective. I've taken them on whatever lure I've been fishing at the time. It is merely a matter of good and careful presentation technique.

Yes, watching the trout can be productive. It can give you confidence in knowing where the trout are so that you can fish with more decision. When you are able to spot their feeding times and recognize what they are taking, you will be in a better position to give them what they want when they want it. You won't be playing blind man's chuck-and-chance-it any more.

# 2
# Drama of the Evening Rise

This is the show that trout fishermen wait for.

The evening rise can be the most exciting and productive time of an angler's hours astream. Yet the question often arises: Why weren't more than a very few fish, out of a pool boiling over with trout, put into the creel—or at least hooked and released? The dry-fly angler can hardly miss taking fish sometime during this brief period when the trout are actually feeding on the surface, but the wet-fly and nymph fisherman has the better odds.

In this chapter we see the closing acts of that drama. The sky darkens and more of the big trout cruise the calmer areas as they venture forth from daytime lairs, nosing for flies, hatching nymphs, or blow-ins. The shark-like dorsal fin is the sign of a big one. Fly pattern means less now. You may take trout on a drab Quill Gordon, while your companion has success with a brilliant Royal Coachman.

While the light is running out, trout commence to dimple in quiet waters, perhaps the tail of the pool, when the monsters have been drawn forth for their night feeding. It is a solid but unhurried rise, seldom obvious, often minnowlike. No drag is allowed in presentation on quiet stretches. Drag is used to advantage in others. An extra-fine leader is a must. It is the silhouette of the fly that the trout go for, not a specific color or pattern, but it's a floater for sure.

The brief but exciting last-act ballet of the mayfly spinners as they mate in the air and deposit their eggs by dipping down near or on the surface, generally in the faster water at the head of a pool, elicits the slash and leap. Darkness has taken over; pattern definition is useless. Cast a sparse dry fly over and over again in a stretch where rising fish are showing, letting the fly drift only a foot or two, then recast. It will drive them crazy and help locate the big ones. Then, as suddenly as it started, it's all over.

But, like a great symphony, the theme is established long before the final movement. The ephemeral creatures that are nymphs living on the stream bottom respond to selected stimuli: light, temperature, and certain chemical changes in an obscure watery world. Some of these nymphs crawl, some burrow, and some swim. They are flat and they are near-round. Strong-legged ones will come from the fast water, others will break out of tiny pebbled houses, and still others will rise from distant rocks and tumble from reeds. Yet, all these varied elements blend into one great pulsing rhythm in the half dark known as the evening rise.

A man wearing the tools of an angler justifies his role in the river's symphony by inserting obbligatos of the nervous swim of a hatching nymph, the quiet float of a nubian dun, and the sudden strength of a coming mayfly. These things he creates from feathers and tinsel, wool and steel, guided by the keenness of his eye and the measure of his hand. The trout is master, and the intruder will have to learn his ways. Each of these nymphal movements has been carefully learned by the fish and, we hope, by the angler. This, then, is the test of the fly fisherman—to blend his counterfeits among the players that the trout knows as professionals. How skillfully the angler plays his bamboo over the dark water is only a part of the perfect score.

# 3
# On Fly Tying

Just before this was written I had the privilege of teaching a young man to tie a Royal Coachman wet fly in twenty minutes. The fly wasn't of the quality that one would expect at the local tackle store, but I'll guarantee it'll catch fish.

A few years ago, while engaged in filming a documentary on the Jewish Chronic Disease Hospital in Brooklyn, N.Y., I chanced to be talking with the doctors and therapists and next day appeared on the scene with my fly-tying equipment.

I was introduced to a patient afflicted with Parkinson's disease. He had the "shakes" so bad that it was pathetic. He had once been a fly fisherman, though he had never tied flies. I sat down with him and gently held his hands through all the steps of tying a simple bucktail. Then, I merely guided him along in the session as he was tying his own fly. Never once did he shake during the performance. He never got to fish with that bucktail, but it is one of the most valuable flies that he (or I) have ever touched. Later, I learned that he was teaching other patients.

At the New York Sportsmen's Shows, we used to set up a big booth and long tables and chairs for fly-tying lessons. People came in droves to try their hands, and usually in one evening we were able to send them home with the right equipment, the basic steps learned, and patterns to follow. It was exciting to see so many people of all ages take part in the art, or hobby, or whatever you call it.

I once had a good friend who was an acute alcoholic. But when he became turned on to the attention that is required to tie a fly, he forgot the need for his favorite restorative. It was only after the equipment was packed away and he had returned to the usual mechanicalness of his well-crystallized life pattern that he required a drink. For years he "drank" fly tying and recovered from the illness before he died.

While on a fishing trip I met a young man who had fished all his younger years but had had one arm shot off as a result of trying to save the world in the war. After three sessions at the tying vise he was able to tie flies—good ones. He's been selling them ever since.

Arthur Mills, of Mills Tackle Store in New York, the oldest in the United States, was shopping around the trade, including the foreign markets, for good flies to sell his selective customers. When I suggested that he start a fly-tying group at the Mills rod factory, he took me up.

"Give me twelve women who have had some experience in sewing or knitting and the like, and I'll have three of them tying for you commercially in three weeks," I said.

We did it and with a comfortable margin. The project was the difficult Royal Coachman fan-wing fly, especially the way he insisted it be done.

More recently, I've been teaching fly tying and lecturing on the subject on the West Coast and attending fly-tying classes put on by the FFF member clubs in the Los Angeles area. I always find it gratifying if I can get a newcomer well started.

Fly tying is fast and easy. Good fly tying takes a little longer. The artist develops as quickly as his talents and abilities become tuned to the sensitiveness of routine, perfection, and inventiveness. I can count among best friends and acquaintances at least twenty-five flytiers of varying

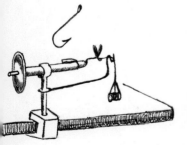

abilities and qualities. I know one doctor who has been tying flies for years and has never fished! He ties for relaxation. His creations are as accurate and distinctive and perfect as his operations on human beings.

Throughout the years that I've spent squinting behind a fly-tying vise, I've had the fun of knowing and learning from many experts. I can remember the first evening spent in the dusty Angler's Roost tackle store in New York's Chrysler Building, as masterminded by Jim Deren. In those days the famed Scottish flytier, Liz Greigg, used to come in and tie and teach. I watched her in amazement, sitting there next to the fly-tying table while a student, maybe an executive of a corporation or a newsboy, was trying his hand. All the while Liz was coaching him she would be tying a difficult wet-fly pattern, such as the Black Dose, by hand and as easily as a nervous woman can twist a handkerchief. And she could tie 20s—drys—in the same fashion! Jim was no slouch, either. When he'd get going, he'd come up with fly patterns tied to perfection, flies I was proud to own. His Fifty Degrees, tied for the Beaverkill in May, is a good example.

There was quite a coterie of tiers that frequented the Roost in those days: Alex Rogan, one of the best and least celebrated, could tie salmon flies that equal British tradition; Ed Sens, my mentor, responsible for many of the patterns featured in my various books, a meticulous German who tied to match his personality; Don Leyden; Ralph Ortopf; Charles DeFeo, both artist and tier; Ray Camp, and Ray Trullinger, both New York newspaper outdoor columnists and excellent tiers and fishermen; and Stu Longendyke, who among other contributions, tied flies for book photography. Artist-tier, the late Don Ray, was a habitue of the Roost as was his pal, Larry Koller, one of the best flytiers this author has ever studied under.

Further afield, I milked many experts for their knowledge: Harry and Elsie Darbee and the Walt Dettes on the Beaverkill, Ray Smith and the Fokert brothers on the Esopus; Edward Hewitt on the Neversink; and Art Flick on the Schoharie; and, by mail, George Skues of England traded samples and letters on the art of tying nymphs with me, a few years before he died. Then there were the times I've stood watching over the shoulder of Ernie Schwiebert and my old friend the late John Atherton on his favorite water, the Battenkill in Vermont. Wow —what tiers!

And I can't mention 'em all, there's not enough space. You'll find 'em in the best trout and game fish waters—hundreds of them.

The point here is that the learning goes on, never ending. One can always pick up a pointer in technique, material usage, and color blending from a fellow tier. In recent years I spent quite a bit of time with the late Mark Kerridge in Fullerton, California. While he was not a professional tier, he tied up enough stock for his friends. It was inspiring to watch an old pro like Mark. He put his heart into it. Ever fiber of his flies reflected the fish and the streams and parts of the world in which he had fished.

Now, the reason for all this background is to point out that all of us had to start somewhere, some time. I may be a well-tempered author of fishing books and fly tying, but a famous tier? No. In order to become famous, one has to desire to produce flies that are handed to the experts, who in turn make you famous. Then there's the business of self-promotion that can make fame but not better tying.

I'd like to point out here that there is a great difference between a tier who can, without worrying about time, turn out flies that should be mounted on plaques, they are so beautiful, and the artisan-craftsman who can tie by the hundreds as the means of making a living.

Over in England the women who tie flies for Hardy, the finest in the world, take years to become top professionals. You can drop a dozen Hardy dry flies of a single pattern on the glass of a counter top, pick one up, examine it, and throw it back into the pile and never find it again because they are all identical—and perfect. Few who read this book will become classic tiers of that ilk, nor is it required. But fly tying to perfection is an art. As a craft and business it can make you money and perhaps, if you want to promote yourself, make you famous.

One of the most rewarding experiences I know is to tie a fly and then go out and catch a fish with it. Never mind whether or not it will sell on the tackle counter or impress magazine editors. That can come later if you desire.

There are many basic books available for instruction. Study each step and master each one before going on to the next. Don't try to tie a completed fly in the first hour or even the first night. Take it easy. If you learn each step perfectly and can perform it easily, almost in a second-nature routine, then you are on your way. The basics are standard, only the materials change and the fly styles. Tying in the material and making it stay where you want it to stay are also essential.

One word of warning: Follow the directions and stick to the pattern of steps from the layout of materials and hooks right to the finish. Learn the right way to do it. Then, if you develop shortcuts or alternate ways to tie, all well and good.

Also, to learn the traditions of the art, study the famous patterns. Tie them just as the material list and style calls for. Then, later, if you cannot always find the exact materials, you can substitute equally effective mixtures. Follow the trend in tying, and note, for example, that most American tiers are getting away from the divided duckwing wings prescribed for most English or American-English style flies. They are now using more hairwings. Many patterns that call for fur are being discarded for the more floatable flosses and quill bodies.

Where specific hackle is required, it is often possible to blend two or three hackles of varied colors in order to get the same effect. The blue-dun hackle is a case in point and is hard to obtain even with money.

It is also advised not to go out and buy a great deal of material at first just in order to tie a particular list of flies.

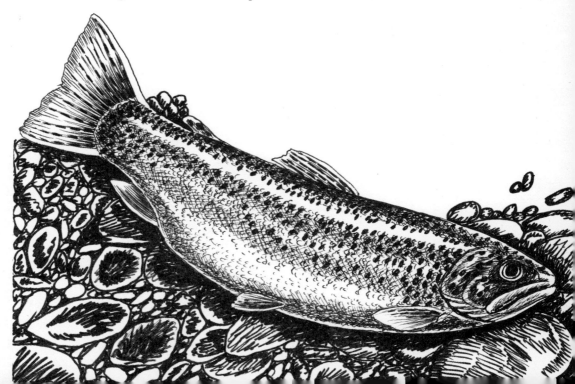

Start with the basic materials list shown in the text you've chosen. That will be sufficient for learning and tying usable flies. Then, when you desire to augment your material supply and are organized to keep all these materials in order, it is time to go on a buying spree. Many, many of the materials used in most flies can be had by visiting the local furrier, dry goods counters, and secondhand stores. Worn out furs make a veritable prize. I once picked up a whole polar bear skin with a few moth holes in it for five dollars! Nothing is sacred—even the hairs on the family dog. And if you are a hunter, many of the most-used feathers come from your ducks and upland game birds, and you can coax your friends to donate their bucktails in exchange for some of your flies.

# 4
# The Fly and the Angler

May the rods of Swisher and Richards always bend to a fighting fish and the light never go out over their fly-tying vise. Their contribution of the no-hackle fly to angling is a step forward and I, for one, salute it.

But it is interesting that sometimes ideas are born twins. The principle of the wheel, for example, was reputedly discovered in several places at the same time in different parts of the earth.

I can remember one birthday of mine, many years ago. Dad had just returned from Europe and with him, as usual, were gifts that only a fly-fisherman could enjoy. Seems he had been fishing in France with one of his financial contacts. The angler was either a good flytier or knew someone who was. In previous years Dad had brought over some excellent dry flies from England, but this time he had something different: a dry fly with no hackle. I was quite intrigued. That summer during our vacation at our camp in New Brunswick, I tried them out on the native brook trout. They caught fish.

Over many years, I eventually forgot about the dozen hackleless flies from the land of l'amour.

I think I'd been tying flies for about ten years when one

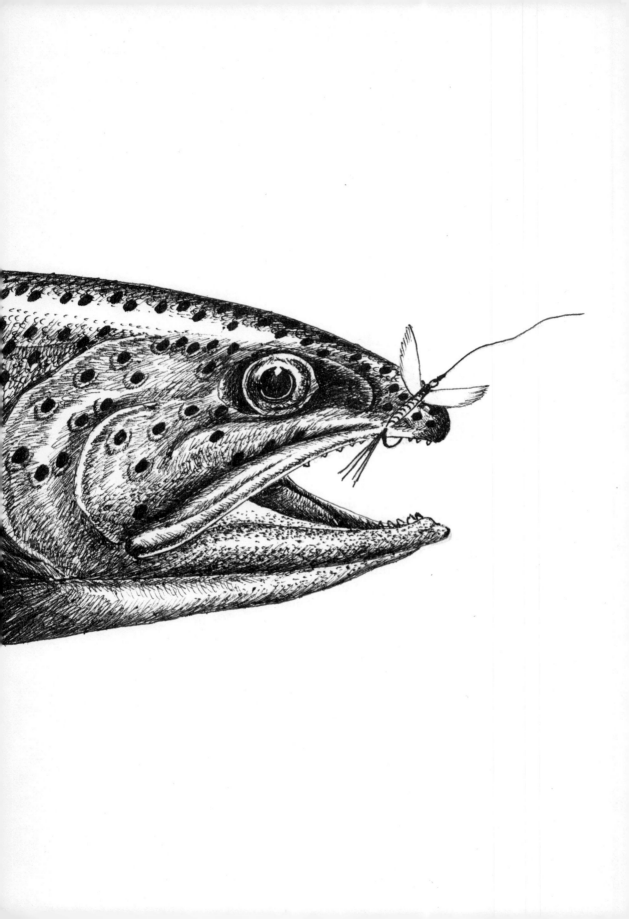

night I had to tie up a flock of flies for a trip to begin the next morning. I collected all the ones I'd tied (even some rejects) and sat down to tie a few more. That night I was really with it when it came to cocking the wings. So I tied a half dozen flies up to the point of the wings and left them on the bench while I went off to conjure a kitchen snack.

DUCK WING

Something or other happened, and I never returned to the vise. Next morning, being in a hurry, I automatically scooped up the flies, plopped them into a spare little box, stuck the box in my jacket, and was off with a double clutch, spewing gravel over the petunias.

It was only after I'd driven the first fifty miles that my memory bank cranked up a photo for my inner viewing screen. I'd tied hackleless dry flies. And they were just like the ones Dad had brought over from France twenty or so years before. I could hardly wait to put them to work. Sure, the French flies had taken brook trout in New Brunswick, but how would these ultra-sophisticated, wary, particular, and skittish browns of the Beaverkill react to my flies?

FAN WING

After I arrived at Roscoe, N.Y., and looked up my old fishing pal, we had a good breakfast, and it was over that last cup of coffee that I produced from my jacket the little box with the hackleless flies. John looked at them, a bit surprised at first. He peered over his glasses at them, turned them over in his fingers, bounced them around on the table top, picked a couple of them up, peered over his glasses at me, put them back into the box, and asked, "What happened? You forget to put their pants on? They look absolutely nude!"

FUR WING

"Yeah," I said. "They do look a bit undressed, John, but you know what?"

"No. What?"

Then I told him the story I told you just now.

"Well," he said, "let's give 'em a whirl."

"Okay. Just maybe. . . ."

Well, sir, those flies were the hit of the day. On the first few casts, we took trout and nice ones. Conditions were just right and a hatch of Quill Gordons came off about eleven o'clock that morning, and we had a ball with the little gray flies.

DOWN WING

So, we never fished with anything else that day—that is, until we ran out of the flies. That night I tied up a bunch

WINGLESS

BIVISIBLE

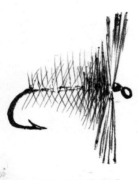

PALMERED BIVISIBLE

of them, and at the rooming house where we were staying, some other anglers became enthusiastic and wanted some. So, naturally, I tied up a storm.

When we came into town for refreshment, we stopped by Harry Darbee and showed the flies to him. He looked them over casually and handed them back to me with the remark, "So what else is new?"

Then, for some reason, I tied very few of those flies and up until the debut of the great book by Swisher-Richards, I haven't tied one. Their book shows an obvious improvement in the tying procedure, and they've come up with what appears, to the angler at least, to be a better fly. With a generation of fly-fishermen starving, evidently, for something new, the founts of the publishing industry have burst forth with a whole new menu of dry flies which is great for the smorgasbord! These authors have written in detail about this type of fly and the endless justifications for its existence. Perhaps the old boy in France who tied them up almost fifty years ago is spinning in his grave. We salute him too.

Since then, because of the exotic attraction of the flies that Dad had given me for my birthday, I have used them with gusto and perseverance. Now that the hackleless fly has been formally established across the land, I shall go forth with countless buddies across the nation and fish with them. We'll all catch fish with them, too, and I suspect that it was for the same reason that the Mickey Fin bucktail became such a demanded fly at the tackle counter. Before John Alden Knight wrote about it, you couldn't sell 'em for beans. But with enough fishermen using them, how could you lose?

## Wingless Fly

When Edward R. Hewitt developed the bivisible fly, he not only made a staunch contribution to flies that would catch trout, but he eliminated one of the worst problems of dry-fly fishing: trying to see the fly under difficult light conditions. The sparse ring of white hackle in front of the basic wingless fly made it visible in darkness, under tricky water lights, and in reflections. This was a real contribution. Even the white-winged flies failed to have the same visibility as the shiney hackles that picked up whatever light was available. If the flies never caught any more trout than the conventional patterns, his contribution is a monument to ingenuity. Praises.

It is a simple fly to tie. In the form he fashioned it, it is tied on a short shank hook and starting from the tail, palmer-tied forward to the eye, leaving enough space for the insertion of two or three turns of white hackles which should be just a tiny bit longer than the ones behind it. The fly floats on an angle pointing upwards. Whether this is good or bad is a point to reckon with.

A variation of the fly is one tied with conventional tail and any style body: fur, ribbed, quill, or whatnot. The hackle is bunched in tight and the wings are absent. Then, in front, the few turns of white. This fly tends to alight and ride even with the water unless the hackles are too long. Both are easily visible and both catch fish. Basic colors run from black to white and multicolors, with the white predominating.

These flies were quite popular in the East in the forties, and many tackle companies such as Weber added them to their catalogues. The mail-order houses promoted them to the anglers, and local tackle counters had them as tied by local tiers. Hardly an angler worth his salt would go astream without at least a fair assortment, and he used them in good and bad light.

You don't read much if anything about the wingless fly. Publishers and editors are constantly looking for something new. It's like the music business. Time was when a Gershwin tune was always a top tune, a standard. In those days there were not too many tunes coming out and much fewer records were being made. Today in our consume-and-replace economy, a new tune and a new group appears on the scene, skyrocketing to fame and dying out, with five new ones on its heels to enjoy the same sudden blossoming. Only time tells the truth. The good ones become standards. Perhaps only one out of a thousand. A masterpiece is never enjoyed by its maker as such, only by those who follow and discover it, or like the hackleless fly, REdiscover it and bring it back into the light.

I recently made a survey of fly trays in several stores and inquired of several mail-order houses that sell flies by the gross. NONE of them marketed the bivisible. It is passé, but I predict that in a few years some bright flytier will rediscover it and once again the ghost creation of Hewitt will float again.

## Four-Winged Fly

Most inventive flytiers are characterized by their waywardness from the conventional. This tier is no exception. Once, while studying tied flies floating over the waters of a swimming pool, I noticed something that I thought should be particularly attractive to a trout. One of the dry flies, by motion of the waves, had become inverted, with the wings poking the surface film in a most obvious way. This rather intrigued me, so one night at the vise I tried tying a fly with four wings, just to see what it would look like and also to find out what problems there would be in making the fly well balanced.

First I tried duckwing sections, tying the usual two uprights in place and then attempting to tie in the two bottom ones in the same space on the shank. (See illustration.) After several tries, I was able to come up with a fly that might be considered presentable. Then I tried wood-duck flank feather fibers, such as are assigned to the Hendrickson pattern. These seemed better; so I then proceeded to hackle the four wings with just a few turns, enough to complete the conventional hackle and wing style.

These flies cast well, though there was more resistance in the wind, somewhat comparable to the fan-wing style. But they did cast well and, what is more important, they floated extremely well. The two out-of-water wings were there for me to see and the lower two poked through the surface film for the benefit of the trout. All I needed now was to try them out in action.

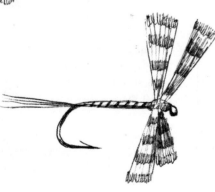

It was about a month later when I was finally able to get to my favorite river and cast them. Up to this point, I had not told anyone about what would have probably been deemed a heresy. Only hooked trout would prove their worth.

The Bridge Pool at Phoenicia on the Esopus was the laboratory. There was a fine hatch of dark Hendricksons on the water, and some fish could be seen rising intermittently.

As was my custom during experimenting on patterns, I tied on a conventional dark Hendrickson with only two wings on the end of the fine tippet and on a branch of the leader I tied on the new creation. The first three trout that rose to my cast came up under the conventional fly. I didn't hook any of them in that particular riff. Wading up a few feet into some faster water, I again cast the two flies and watched them float through the glaze of ripply light and glare. A sudden splash erupted between them, and I felt the strike of a heavy trout but didn't yet know which fly he'd taken. As I brought him into the net I noted with some pride that he had taken the four-winged fly. While this was a proof of some sorts, it was hardly enough to become elated over.

I waded ashore and headed for Folkert's store and showed both the trout and the fly to Dick, who is a brother in this experimenting business. He looked the fly over carefully, bounced it on the glass counter. Then I produced six more flies that had not as yet been wetted. "Try these with me tonight, Dick. Maybe we have something of interest here."

At sundown that evening we fished the big pool side by side. The trout were rising all over the place to something but not to our patterns. Neither of us caught anything.

Several weeks went by before I was again able to experiment with the four-wing fly or any fly for that matter. Finally, another two days of freedom presented themselves and off I went to the river. Naturally, I had tied a couple of dozen four wingers down to size 18, just in case the late season hatches of small mayflies were on the water. Using a four-wing, Pale Evening Dun, I took five small trout, one after the other, all in one part of the center current where there was a hatch of flies coming off the water. I switched to a Pale Evening Dun with only the conventional two wings and caught three more trout before the hatch had subsided and the trout went down for the evening.

Then I became bold enough to pass around a few samples of the flies to several darn good trout fishermen-tiers and asked them to try them and to attempt to tie them with the idea of perfecting a technique which would produce a decent-looking and good-floating fly. Most of them eliminated the hackle, believing that the four wings were enough, with a wooly body and stiff tails.

The results were good. They caught trout with them. But for many years before, they had caught trout without them. And, if they had returned to the two-winged fly, they are probably still catching trout.

All of which proves. . . ?

Without a Swisher-Richards type of deep research and much publicity and a darn good book, the four-winged fly will probably remain on the list of almost-rans.

Perhaps you will take up where I've left off and produce a winner. If nothing else, you'll have fun tying this kind of concoction . . . and, really, isn't that what it's all about?

Probably a gold-ribbed Hare's Ear will do just as well—or better.

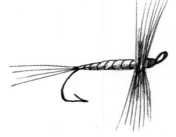

SPACE TIE

USUAL

CENTER TIE SALMON

CROSS-TIE

ADD SHORT HACKLE

## Spiders

I don't know of more than about five flytiers from whom you can buy good spiders. And when you can find them, they'll be expensive no matter what the value of the dollar is. So there's no use in telling you of my experiences and recommendations about how and when to fish the spider unless you have *good* ones in hand.

In order to have them, you'll have to tie them yourself, unless you have midnight access to Harry Darbee's fly-tying kit or to Jimmy Deren's private collection that he keeps behind a secret panel in his living-room bar.

Finding the hackles for tying the spider is most difficult. The way these plumbers cut neck hackles shouldn't happen. They often cut away the neck and leave the feathers that lie on the side of the neck on the dead bird. Those side hackle feathers are priceless. Many cocks do not have more than three or four such feathers, and if they are webby, they are no good.

Saddle hackle feathers, the ones that run down the back of the rooster, are *never* included in the neck for some strange reason. Perhaps it is because the fly-tying dealers can sell those long feathers at a premium. Anyhow, good stiff saddle hackles are also hard to find.

Why all this? Well, if the fly looks good as it comes from the vise and the hackles fold back softly after the first couple of casts, the fly won't be worth a damn.

First of all, there is a proper way to cast the spider. Given an excellent one, excessive and fast false casting will wear out the delicate fibers before the fly even touches the water. Repeated false casting and dragging of the fly through the water will ruin even the best. So you have to learn to respect this diamond and treat it like you'd treat your best friend. Cherish it and only cast it when you mean business.

Do not tie it on a thick leader. Tie it on a very thin length of tippet. It won't act properly on a stiff leader, and you never want it to land straight out, anyway. You want slack in the leader. Also, the softer tippet will not unnecessarily pressure the fly in the cast or through the water. Also, don't expect to cast the spider a country mile.

It is a fly to be dappled. A long cast will be out of place because if the fly is far from the control of the rod it will be impossible to impart the action desired on it to entice the trout. The longest cast should not exceed forty feet and even thirty-five is better. Sacrifice the trout that's fifty feet away or throw something else at him or wade quietly and slowly over to his position.

When false casting the fly to gain your direction, do so *gently,* slowly, and easily . . . don't zip-zip-zip through the air. It will end up being a streamer fly. Cast slowly, directing the fly well off the water and, just as the fly is about to land on the water, raise the rod tip as high as you can reach to keep a minimum of line on the water. Use a long rod if you are going to fish this fly. It is worth changing to the longer rod for such fishing, for spider fishing is a separate art and justifies the proper gear for it.

When the fly alights, roll cast an extra length of leader upstream so there's plenty of slack. The current will move that fly about generously.

Now, the spider is not built to cock upright in the manner of a conventional dry fly. It can land any which way and with a slight breeze and leader slack, freedom can be

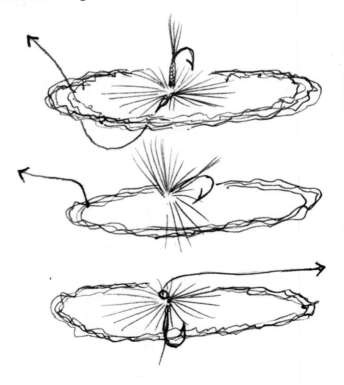

utilized to keep that fly moving. A slight twitch of the rod and lifting of at least some of the leader off the water allows the fly to move and be alive. That's the point of the spider.

I don't quite know why it is called a spider, except perhaps it imitates a spider walking across the water. It is used at any and all times when the angler believes that a fly with life and motion will coax up those pesky dreamers that lie beneath the surface. An active spider can reach their adrenals where it will do the most good.

Manipulation of the spider to give it life can be done in a number of ways. The short mend and roll-pickup cast are good medicine. This will lift the fly off the water gently and place it a few inches or a foot or two if needed upstream for a little better position or drift. I like to cast the spider to the side of a break in the current, even though the chances are that the trout is lying underneath the break. He'll see it out there in the clear and will go for it. A spider cast into bubbling and rough water will tend to bog down and have to be recast too quickly.

Given a slight breeze on the water, the spider really takes on the motions of a living insect. That life motivates the trout, and I believe that it doesn't make a particle of difference whether it imitates a spider, wind-blown land insect, or an aquatic that has hatched. It is the motion stimulating the cat-and-mouse sense of the chase built into every trout and bass that has accounted for every one I have ever caught in this manner.

You read a lot about selective trout and the difficulty of presenting a specific fly to a trout feeding on a specific type of insect. Throw a spider in the middle of the party, and the spray will begin to fly.

Keep your casts short, hold that rod high to get as much line and leader off the water as possible, and keep the action going. Don't worry about drag. Drag is a help in this instance.

Downstream dry-fly fishing is easy with the spider. Employ the stop-cast. Throw out a good line, and before it lands on the water, stop it in the air to allow slack to fall upstream from the fly, and just at the point the fly is about to be pulled under, roll-pickup cast the fly so as not to have it dragged underwater and unduly strained. Cast it right back to the same spot and repeat and repeat. If your spot is a good one, the head of a run or the top of a V wake behind a log or rock or underwater drop-off such as a shelving riffle, all the better.

Remember to false cast *slowly* . . . don't wear out that beautiful fly in the air, nor suck it underwater on the retrieve.

Now, to tie that fly. Shown here are the conventional sizes and relative shapes in regard to hook size. The trick in tying these flies demands techniques not necessarily needed in tying the conventional dry fly. First of all, the winding-on of the hackle needs to be strong and under *even* pressure as you wind. If the hackle is slack, the fine strands will tend to lie back on the first casts. Even a prize feather can be wasted by uneven pressure in winding it on the hook. Also, tie the hackles against each other as shown. This gives added strength and floatability.

The second part of the trick is to build up the tying thread around the area of the hackle to form a sort of slot for the stem to sit in (see illustration). The third part of the tying is seldom if ever done and certainly I've never seen anything in writing about it. Once the hackle is tied in and the spider almost ready for the head job, tie in a stiff dry-fly hackle of a much smaller size and wind *behind* the spider hackle as shown in the diagram. This will offer a back rest for the long fibers and will support them far better than nothing at all.

Also, when you dress your fly to float, do so *sparingly*. Do not gob up the fly as is done usually with conventional flies. If you use a grease applied with the fingers, grease only the *ends* of the fibers, not the whole fly. Under most conditions it is even better to fish the fly ungreased, unless you can use a spray-on floatant. But use any of 'em sparingly.

The Neversink Skater, a particular spider, was invented by Edward R. Hewitt to be fished for the touchy browns on the famed Catskill waters. They work exceedingly well on Atlantic salmon as well as all trout.

Fished on a lake when the trout are rising to insects either just under the surface or on it, the spider has another good use, particularly when there is a bit of breeze present.

I can recall . . . But, shucks, you don't need a story here. Produce your own and you will come up with some beauties if you learn to tie and properly use your own spiders.

## Those Damnable Midges

I fished the dry fly many years before I finally took up the insane department of dry-fly artistry called midge fishing. I tied flies for at least five years before even attempting to tie an 18, much less a 22 or 24 fly. Then it was about five more years before I used them to any extent. I'd read a great deal about midge fishing and its glories as expounded by the scribes of angling who touted it as the epitome of fly-fishing art and science. I was impressed by their stature and prowess and admired, yea even envied them, their experiences . . . long, lightest of leaders,

almost untieable flies, and certainly unseeable flies even under the best light conditions.

Then when the fishing was particularly tough—the trout rising to something I couldn't see, anglers taking trout with such miniscule imitations right in front of me—it was either due to my pride, sense of competition, or just plain curiosity that I tried tying on these damnable little notions. It was hard work just getting the miserable leader through the hook, much less getting a decent knot tied that wouldn't break off in my hands.

While casting the midge was no problem, seeing it once it lit on the water was something else. All I could do was to try and follow the leader that was floating (as it should *not*) on the surface. How in the devil you got a leader to sink and at the same time float that microscopic contraption was something far from my capacity. I was impatient. Logic kept telling me that I should quit this nonsense and offer the trout something worth his efforts. But those guys fishing nearby kept taking trout on them and going into raptures. I was missing the boat, but I kept trying.

Finally one afternoon when no one was looking, I resolved to really give those midges their due. I'd fish with them the whole day despite rises to big Drakes or whatever came along. I'd stick to it come hell or high water.

I did.

I cast midges until my arm was sore. I squinted into reflections until my eyes were bloodshot. I kept changing flies when the ones I was using would not float properly, all the time knowing that color couldn't make much difference in a fly this small, or silhouette, or even size. And I didn't catch a thing, until a swarm of tiny no-see-ums bored out over the water. They were about a quarter of the size of the flies I was using—those idiot size 24s. My flies looked like size 10 Royal Coachmen next to them. Splat!

went the cast. Blap! went a trout, and I was fast to him in the first encounter with so small a hook. The long slender leader took up tight in a flash of spray and the battle was on. When that ten incher came in to be released I felt as if I'd crashed through Mach 5 and could come down for the celebration. I hooked and lost three fish right after that, and they were bigger (of course) than the one I hooked. By darkness I'd landed and released ten trout on those midges and I was plumb sold. From then on, I'd fish them as often as conditions called for and even when they didn't. I'd save and savor them for the times conventional-size flies were not turning over the score.

Consequent experimentation and experience with fishing the midge brings the conclusion that here, truly, is the epitome of dry-fly fishing . . . working down as small as you can go, lightest and longest leaders and a rod that is equally fine, spirited, and light.

Of course, a small rod is not necessary for the enjoyment of midging. Just because the fly is small does not mean it requires a small rod to cast it. On the contrary, I like to fish with a nine-foot rod, since I'll have to worry less about distance and can easily raise the rod high in order to have only the leader on the water. From this position a simple and very easy forward roll-pickup cast will dance the fly up and off the water and at that same instant I relax the rod and drop the fly down again. Repeating this performance many times in quick succession brings trout to the surface even if they were not feeding on midges. They come to the little fly in many cases much quicker than they would to a larger fly.

As to whether they take this little guy as a direct imitation of a midge larva about to hatch or the hatched fly or as an imitation of any sort of fly, land-bred or aquatic, is still an unresolved point in my book. Just because the fly is tied to imitate a midge or mosquito larva is no sign that it is taken by the trout to be the truth. Just why the trout seem to go for midges is still an up-in-the-air question with me.

That's why I like to fish with them. Certainly, the smaller the pattern the less the trout is likely to find out the fraud. That's the prime reason, in my opinion, why trout seem to go for midges when all else fails.

During the conditions when spinners of mayflies are on

the water and duns of an evening hatch are intermingling with them, it is practically impossible to try and match up the flies in the box with the desires of the trout. You can go crazy trying to do that. For this situation I have two cures, one the variant mentioned elsewhere and the damnable little midge.

But midging gets tough as it gets dark. And the darker it gets, the better is the midging. But don't get caught in that light with a bare leader when you have struck too hard and left the fly with the fish. You'll have to tie on another, and it's a pesky problem to tie one on in a glare from the water at sunset or in the darkness that is accentuated by the shadows thrown at you from the overhanging foliage.

Trout like them . . . and so do the bats. I've hooked bats, swallows, and one kingbird with midges, and that's one good way to shake you into a heart attack and break the fine tip of your rod.

You've got to be a real nut to seriously consider midge fishing, but once taken in with at least a modicum of success you become a specialist.

And you know something strange? They take trout at all seasons of the year. I've fished midges in April when the trout were not even interested in the Quill Gordons or Iron Blue Duns. I've taken trout when they were feeding on Greek Drakes in the middle of the afternoon.

Tying them is simple. On the opposite page are some of mine that seem to work pretty well for me.

The midge does one thing more for you. It shows that the smaller the fly, the better chances of fooling him. Tie up some legit mayfly patterns on size 20 hooks, and try them next time the trout are hitting light or not at all. You'll be surprised.

## Spinners and Variants

As any trout knows, the food value in a spinner mayfly is of little importance. It is like eating dehydrated and devitaminized breakfast food. There's more nutrition in a cardboard box. So why do the trout make such a fuss when the spinners are on the water, usually during twilight and into the evening?

Well, the life story of the mayfly includes the nymphal

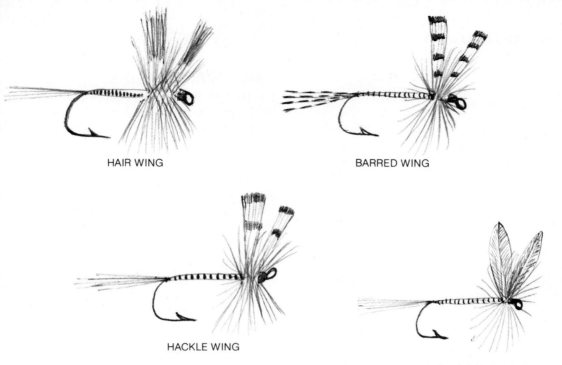

HAIR WING

BARRED WING

HACKLE WING

HACKLE POINT WING

stage when it grows underwater, hanging on to the rocks, gravel, and refuse of the stream bottom or burrowing in the comfortable mud of the slack portions of the stream. When it comes time to emerge as a dun, it drifts in the current, slowly lifting itself to the surface where it casts its nymphal "wet suit" and pops out its wings, floats as a dun on the water, and if no trout or song bird gets it, it flies to the nearest branch or rock, rests a bit, begins to undress, and in a few hours transforms into the adult or spinner stage.

EGG SAC

As a dun it had already quit feeding. It is living on earned income. Now, as a spinner, its final burst of life, it has but one purpose: to breed and continue the race. This it does in a magnificent dance over the water as it looks for its mate. You've probably noticed insects zigzagging up and down over the water. Those are mayfly spinners mating. The female will shortly develop an egg cluster at the base of her abdomen next to the tail. *This* is what the trout look for: a dainty bit of highly concentrated food. The green puffball at the end of the Royal Coachman offers this silhouette, as does the yellow egg sac on the female Beaverkill (which is also an imitation of the female caddis fly).

SPENT WING

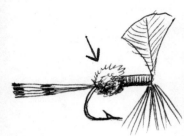

When the mayflies finish their ritual, they die. But before this, the females dip down to the water surface, and the eggs are knocked off by the impact. The dead mayflies lie in spent-wing fashion on the water and the trout gorge themselves on them.

If you are fishing with a knotted tapered leader you'll likely feel dainty "tips" on the leader and wonder what's up. If you can look closely and see the action, it is trout bumping the knot on the leader. I fished for a number of years before I was able to discover why they were doing that during the evening and seldom if ever during the day when the spinners were not about.

Ed Sens told me what it was all about, as I have told you here. He even had me snip off the fly I was using and tie a couple of knots at the end of my leader.

"Cast that out and you'll see what I mean," he coached.

"Well, I'll be," I said, getting a sizeable bump.

That night I tied up some size 20 hooks with three turns of ten-pound mono and tied them off with just a couple rounds of hackle so that they would make some impression on the water. I figured that the hackle would also help the new idea stay afloat. I took trout on them. Nice ones.

Then I refined the fly a bit, using yellow and gray yarn mixed evenly and twisted on a little bump in the center of the hook and pulled out the hairs just a bit, skipping the hackle. Dressed this way with fly dope and again . . . the creation took fish.

Then I got to thinking about the variant flies I'd been tying for the spinner hatch. I'd never thought of tying the egg sac to the rear of the fly.

My spinner variants are all effective *only in the evening* and when there is a sizeable flight of spinners in the air and on the water.

The flies are exceptional, including the spent-wing variation. I also use a variant with white hackle wings for the last few casts before darkness sets in. I can see this fly a bit better than the drab spinners. I can never see the little egg sac job, so I usually attach a teaser puffball white dry fly up about a foot from the end of the leader. It also acts as a "bobber."

The particular variant I tie employs neither hairwing

nor hackle-point wing, but long hackle fibers tied with a V cut in the center to make the fly conform to convention. Then I add hackle a bit shorter to fit the fly size. My spinners are, as you can see, almost spider-fly dimension. I fish them often in place of spiders, even during the day, especially if I have only a few spiders in the box.

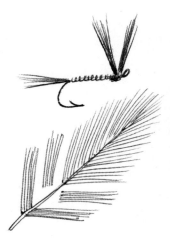

Shown here is the female caddis fly sporting the egg sac. She drops down to the water in much the same way as the mayfly, and they descend in droves.

About the only time this type of fly is not killing is on an evening, especially in midseason when there are several species of flies hatching *in the evening* at the same time the spinners of yesterday are returning to lay their eggs. Chances are that the duns of the hatch will attract the eyes and appetites of the trout, and if they become selective to those duns, they most likely will only take a spinner by accident or casually.

This condition does not exist during the evenings of the early Quill Gordon or even the Hendrickson or March Brown; but the confusion period is when the Cahills and Pale Evening Duns are about. That mixture really adds zest to the job of finding just what the trout would like for dinner.

I can recall two instances of record.

In the first case I was fishing with the conventional light Cahill fly since they were beginning to show on the water. The trout were rising all over the pool. That afternoon when I had first entered the pool, you would have thought there was not a trout within miles. But as evening approached. . . .

In the confusion of all those insects, including a generous hatch of caddis, I stuck to my guns with the light Cahill. Trout would bust all around me and more than once I struck, believing that they were hitting my fly. But my score was zero.

I fished the same fly for a half hour more and still no action. I was about to change flies but didn't know what to change to. Another cast and a big brown snuffed the fly and headed down the center of the pool. The other trout were so actively feeding that he didn't even disturb them. After I unhooked and released him I blew on the fly and sent it on its way again. Another hit and another trout. In fifteen minutes I had taken and released twelve trout, all of good size, and one whopper that went fifteen inches—a good trout for that stream, in fact, an excellent one. And all this happened when I could plainly see the spent spinners and their egg sacs drifting by me.

On another evening, I took out my new variants with the yellow egg sac loaded onto the stern. I cast these for an hour and was about to change over to the Cahills, since they were abundant. The same story. All at once, the trout seemed to shift over from one goodie to another, and I was able in a few short minutes to catch my breakfast.

So, a great deal of experimentation can be done in this area of spinners, spent-wing spinners, and the little egg-sac pattern.

I do not limit the use of the variants to strictly evening or twilight fishing. A variant is a variant and often can be used for a fish finder when no hatches are going on and no drifting insects can be seen on the water. Being variant, they are multicolored and not too prominent in silhouette, making it a possible argument for a vague type of insect to coax trout up with, rather than offering a distinctive fly of a certain pattern.

I've taken trout with the variant when even the minnows were not playing in the shallows and not a bird was over the water looking for their winged food. Everything was quiet. Yet, the variant paid its way.

So, if in doubt, have a supply of them in the fly box —tied sparse and in varied shades from black and black-brown-gold to pink and gray, olive and gray, olive and tan, with quill bodies of similar coloration. Use the wisp of white hackle as mentioned before when the darkness begins to creep out over the water.

Fish these flies at the heads of pools, for that's where the action usually starts. But before you leave for the night, take a walk down to the tail of the pool and wade as quietly as possible and shoot a long one out as far as you can to a current rip. The big browns that have avoided all the action to this time will be working their way upstream from their lairs in the tail runs. They'll be there to watch out for minnows, too, but you'll likely hit into a big brown cruising around just looking for a battle.

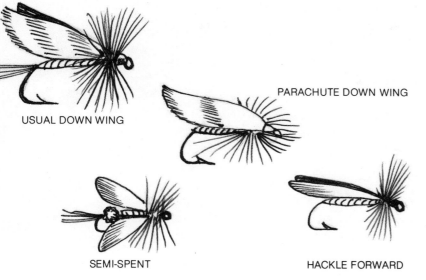

USUAL DOWN WING

PARACHUTE DOWN WING

SEMI-SPENT

HACKLE FORWARD

## *Merits of the Down-Wing Dry Fly*

Too much attention has been given to the imitation of the mayfly. While this species is one of the most dominant of the aquatics and makes up a featured portion of the trout's diet, there are other little bugs about that sometimes are of more importance.

Caddis flies are a case in point. In many of our streams where the mayfly hatches are growing less and less, the caddis fly seems to make out very well and in some cases is on the increase.

Caddis, for the most part, hatch in veritable droves; clouds of them cover the water, fill the air, alight on your rod tip, your line, your hand, your eyeglasses, hatband, and particularly the back of your neck. Fortunately they do not bite! And the trout go absolutely nuts during such a snowstorm of edible goodies.

And you can cast and cast the conventional up-wing dry fly and be lucky if you get a tumble, much less a good solid rise. Yet, stomach analysis of a caught trout will reveal that the stomach is filled to the gills with these little insects.

CADDIS

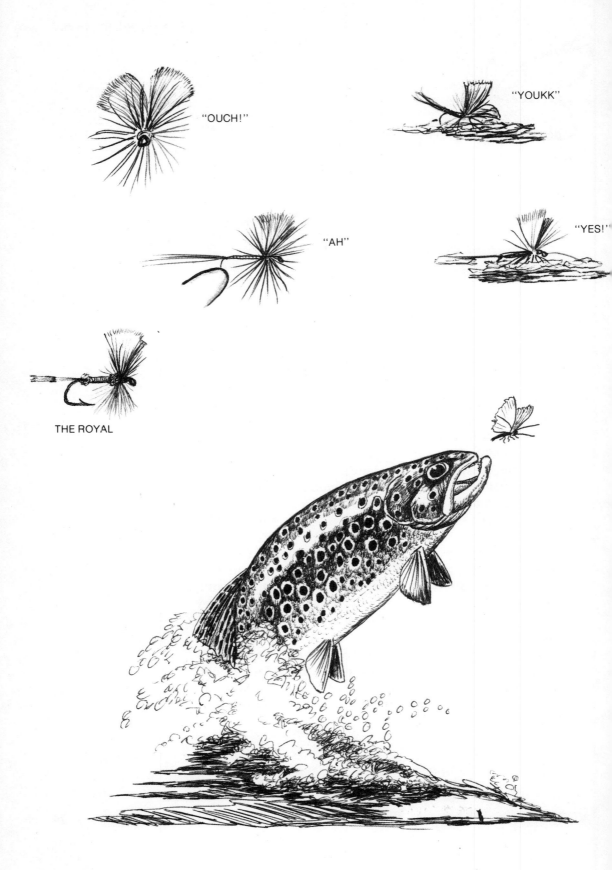

Look at these and make up your own imitations. Of course the conventional down-wing wet fly is often taken by trout, I'm sure, as the imitation of the caddis, but you see few fly boxes with down-wing dry flies in them. If you do, they are of the conventional shape as shown here. Look mine over and tie up a few.

## Butterflies, Fan Wings, and Big Brown Trout

Summer. A hot August day. Faint sporadic breezes. No insects on the water. Even the kingbirds and phoebes were hidden somewhere. Not a minnow was stirring.

Upstream, the long broad pool was glistening and shimmering as the currents poured down from the boulders, and white water gradually flattened out into unidentifiable currents over the pool's deep that passed by me where I was wading.

I was purposefully in waist-deep in order to keep cool, moving along slowly as is my custom. Looking down, I could see trout nosing around in the gravel, and some lined up behind me in my wake.

Once in a while, a slight breeze would filter down the valley to cool the brow and ruffle the water. Sometimes leaves would be blowing high over the pool to settle on the surface and glide by me like little boats on a calm but moving sea.

My senses were tuned to the routine of casting, and as I proceeded slowly up toward the head of the pool I was entirely unmindful of what I was doing. Years of casting habit were placing the line gently and purposefully upcurrent, sometimes directly upstream, at other times to the side of the pool or out over the central current. It was relaxing just to be there watching my automatic mechanism doing so well.

Then, a sudden puff of wind, some leaves in the air, and directly ahead of my floating fly, a bright yellow butterfly fluttered erratically across the stream, dipping dangerously close to the surface one second, only to zoom up into the air and then go down again.

Once it careened down to almost touch my dry fly. At that instant the water silvered beneath it, and the hulk of a big brown trout slipped out of the bubbles, flailing on the momentum of a powerful tail flip, right into the air some two feet over the water. When he dove down under again, the little yellow butterfly was no longer in evidence.

By this time, my size 18 light Cahill, completely ignored and undisturbed, drifted down under the rod tip. I picked it up in my hand, noting that it hardly resembled a yellow butterfly.

I lit a cigarette. Sometimes, in a situation like this, the head can compute a suggestion of what to do and how to proceed. One of my inner voices complained that it was too hot to fish; it was the middle of a summer's day when all trout were napping (or should be) and that anglers should respect this. It maintained that I'd be better off going ashore, resting a while until the shadows began to lengthen over the pool. That voice suggested there would be a return flight of mayfly spinners when the air cooled and quite possibly a hatch of tiny Cahills would come out at dusk. It completely ignored the incident, since mind programming doesn't include this sort of chance happening.

Yet another voice suggested a wild scheme. I've learned to listen to this voice, for it comes up with the darnedest ideas that often produce something. This voice advised me to pick out a fan-wing Yellow Sally, one of the flies that

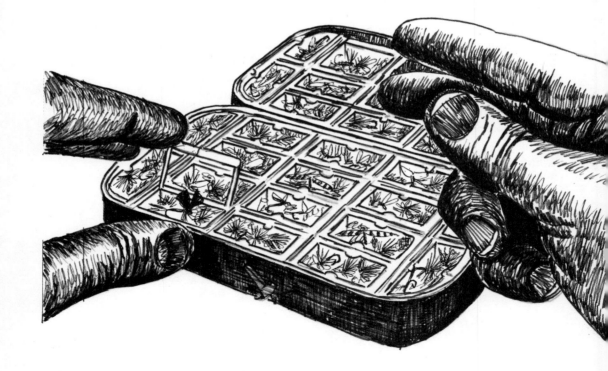

dad had given me years ago from his English collection. Since the day he died, I'd always carried his fly box with me for sentimental reasons, seldom if ever opening it or using the flies.

I fumbled through my fishing vest, found the box, tied on the Yellow Sally, dressed it, and began false casting.

The fly balked somewhat awkwardly as it was being shot out in quick false casts, and I had to slow down and widen my bow. I'd been fishing with an exceptionally long leader tippet, and the fly whirled, flickered, and seemed to dance inches above the water at the end of each false cast. For some reason, I kept false casting the fly, allowing it to soar in near the surface but did not drop it down. It was fun to merely false cast the old fly and watch it spin in the sunshine.

Well, it seemed that someone else was being entertained and on one of the fly's dances and dips down almost to the surface, the water under it suddenly turned to the familiar silvery bubbles, followed by the form of a big brown trout, dorsal fin extended, eeling upwards on its spread tail. He grabbed the fly, whipped the leader and line down under in a rocklike splash.

The shock was one I'd never experienced before or since. My reactions were paralyzed for a fortunate instant. Had I been able to strike, I'd probably have snapped the fly out of the fish's mouth or broken the thin leader.

The brownie must have loved the fight we had, for he came in some minutes later to look me over. He was of a darker color than most browns I'd been seeing; perhaps one of the reputed big ones that I'd heard about that were supposed to inhabit the caverns up under the forbidding boulders and fast water at the head of the pool where flies can never be placed properly.

Yes, he was deep and thick and sported a broad and hooked underjaw, luscious red and black spots and a golden-red belly.

As he swam away under the rod tip, I decided to take the advice of that voice that had said to go ashore. I wasn't quite sure whether or not I'd been dreaming.

Now, on the basis of that experience, I would not take it as a revelation from God and start a new school of fly tying and write a book on a new pattern idea, but I wouldn't forget it either. Obviously it can be classed as exceptional. I've seen many butterflies cross streams and fly enticingly over runs that I've known to contain good fish, but the above experience has not been duplicated.

But, I've since taken many good trout on fan wings. In fact, I always looked with disdain at the Royal Coachman fan wing and considered it one of those British fetishes that could be left out of the fly box. See how our logic has no actual basis in fact. We try to make the trout conform to our ideas and when they do, this compounds our ego while we forget the times that they leave us entirely in the lurch.

Obviously the fan wing can fit into the class of general impressionistic creations, imitating both land-bred and aquatic-bred insects. But where does this leave us? That means that almost *any* crazy or legitimate type of fly could be as good as another, and that all the pattern nonsense is nonsense. We could then go back to one fly, fish it all the time, and probably catch fish. I'd hate to think that this was true!

However, after much experimentation with the fan-wing type of dry fly, I find that it is a most effective fly when the wind lets you alone and distance is not a necessity. In my experimentation I've studied them in contrast to the conventional light Cahill of the same size on the water. It took a neighbor's swimming pool and a face mask to convince me that such study is in order when the neighbors aren't looking. From under the surface, the reflection and light bounce made by the fan wings is stronger and more noticeable to the eye than a conventionally tied wing of, say, duck-feather fibers or even hair-wings, though they come in for second place in the tests. There's something about the fan wing that gives the impression of a fly buzzing its wings.

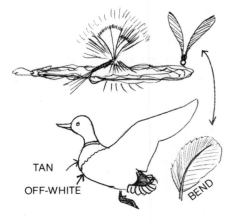

So perhaps the old Britisher who designed the fan wing had some real sense behind his concoction. The popularity of the Royal Coachman fan wing as a beautiful fly is one thing, but when it is tested and proven to be a taker, its reputation lasts.

But, it is hard to get good fan wings. Few tiers know how to proportion the wings correctly, set them properly so that they do not cause undue wind resistance. If the feathers are turned flat to the eye of the hook, they'll be an abomination to cast. If they are not tied in tightly, the wings turn and ruffle up in an unmerciful heap, and the fly does not cock straight upright on the water as it should. But when the correct fly tied on a bit heavier leader than usual is used, it floats like a winning sailboat. Given sufficient leader slack, it can swing around in the current ripples and, by wise and dainty line handling, be made to skip over the surface—like a butterfly or a big fat March Brown mayfly or yellow mayfly flexing its wings after emerging. That'll drive 'em crazy.

The proportions of the fly are also important. It needs a longer, stiffer tail in order to right the position on the water. The hackles need not be thick but of good quality, sparse but much longer than the conventional dimensions recommended by tradition. And since the fly is heavier with such big wings, there is no real need for the usual wool or fur body; the quill or hard body is preferred.

I do not like big fan-wing patterns, that is, tied over size 14. I prefer the size 16 and 18 hooks but with an oversized dimension.

They should be cast upstream conventionally but with a right- or left-hand bend so as to allow the fly to float down without being preceded by the leader. My pickup is always the forward roll cast, not the suck-up kind that will tend to damage the dainty wings.

One other interesting observation: In almost every case of a trout being hooked on a fan wing, *they always take the fly deep in the mouth.* This tells me that they weren't fooling.

I tie a whole series of fan wings for the standard cycle of the season flies are found on most streams. For the Quill Gordon, I make the wings from mallard breast feathers. If I can, I try to obtain "dirty" colors, such as tan, tan-gray, or gray. I use the same wings for the Hen-

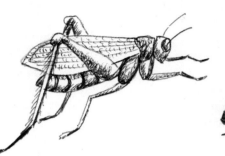

drickson and March Brown. For the Dark Cahill, I try to find a yellow-tan or dye this color, and for the Light Cahill, I prefer the off-white. My Green Drake fan wing is a white mallard breast feather, dyed a pale green—ever so pale.

I like all these flies when I'm fishing the glassy stretches of pools, particularly when there is a hatch upstream and the duns are floating down. When all else fails and I see trout rising—but not to my creation—I fall back on the Royal Coachman. If this fails, and it seldom does, I go ashore and read somebody else's book.

When I go out again to the water, I look for another butterfly incident.

## Land-Bred Insects

Time was when a dozen patterns of dry flies were sufficient and a lot of trout fell for the standard ruses. But, according to the experts, that was in the long, long ago before trout became sophisticated, shy, and extremely selective. Now, it seems that we cannot become astute anglers fishing with the plain old Royal Coachman dry, the Quill Gordon, the Hendrickson, the March Brown, the Gray Fox, the Gingers, Cahills, and Green Drakes . . . goodness, no!

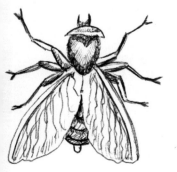

It's the same in wet-fly fishing . . . an angler who hasn't fished all manner of classical nymphs and hasn't developed at least fifty patterns of nymphs, simply isn't in the game.

A few years ago you were behind the times if you were found on the stream or even wore your jacket into the local clubroom without at least one box of Hewitt-type bivisibles. You were shunned as a tyro. Lately, it seems that you can be equally ostracized if you are found lacking the Swisher-Richards, no-hackle flies. It takes a full-time researcher to keep up with the vogue and a manufacturer who is constantly trying to find a place for more pockets for more fly boxes to fulfill his mission.

For a long time a precious few angler-flytiers, particularly in Pennsylvania, were experimenting with the imitation of land-bred insects. Seems the theory was born that the imitation of specific land insects should be mastered for the times in between or after the aquatics had had their season. After all, what would the trout be feeding on after the computer ran out of mayflies and caddis flies and fish flies and mosquitoes and midges and crane flies and Dobson flies and spiders and grasshoppers and moths, and . . . ? A new school was just crying to be started.

Vince Marinaro and Charlie Fox are two of the original culprits. Both came from Pennsylvania and stay there most of the time because their favorite streams are there, and those streams are special streams, too.

It seems that they, and now the rest of us, cannot any longer get along without jassids and other common land breds that choose to fall into the water when other aquatics are not to be had. We must imitate those insects in order to keep on creeling trout when all else is unprogrammed and/or unsuccessful. Seems that these two have discovered that trout can be equally sophisticated and highly selective to land-bred insects as well as aquatics and have gone so far as to write about it in public.

It's a fun game and I'm sure these two serious fishermen take themselves and their newfound toys most seriously. I'd be the last one to condemn a fly that could take trout when all others failed.

But maybe I'm just too old, too over-wise, or just plain lazy, but I cannot yet bring myself to join this school.

True, trout do consume a lot of food that is not aquatic. As a matter of fact, stomach analysis proves beyond a doubt that trout do feed on land-bred insects and that these constitute a major and in some cases the whole diet—particularly in streams which have lost their volume of aquatic hatches. Many of our streams have suffered in past years from severe storms and floods and droughts, and it is a wonder that the trout are still there. We can replace the trout, but we cannot replace the seasonal cycle of aquatic insects. With these in the minority on some streams, the trout must feed on land breds, and I submit that when enough of one species of land bred is on the water and dropping in at a certain time of the year, the trout would naturally look for it. People are like that. When the season is on for watermelon, we go looking for it at the market.

But to where and to what can all this lead? I can visualize the fly-fisher's life in the Brave New World of 2000, when the angler will be burdened by all the fads of the past, the good old standards, and a whole breast pocketful of flies that are designed to imitate these land-bred insects. Since there are probably one hundred times as many land-breds as there are aquatics, I can see our future man going insane trying to collect and match all the drop-ins. Somebody will copy the hatch to make it match the land breds. There'll be a whole catalogue of insects and artificials to match them.

True, I've been guilty of this. I've imitated the little green worm, or caterpillar, that comes out in June in my home waters. It is particularly succulent and attractive to the trout. But I've used any wet fly or floater with a green or green-ribbed, gold-bodied fly when they are around and have taken fish. That the trout took it as the green caterpillar is a point which I am unable to determine. He might have taken it for a caddis fly that wasn't even green. I've also imitated the little yellow moth, or buttercup butterfly, when I've seen them fluttering over the water in the late spring. The age-old Yellow Sally is a perfect imitation in the fan-wing variety. For the grasshopper, of course, any big brown wet fly dappled on the surface or a big Wulff dry fly will suffice for him, and I've seen trout take these with utter abandon when a sudden wind blew hoppers to the pool. And ants . . . ! Trout *love* ants, as bitter and hard as they must be even to the trout gourmet. Little black flies, such as the black gnat or even a plain old wingless all-hackle black fly will suffice here. Who is to know if the trout take them as ants, or something that just looks buggy?

It is something to think about, if you have run out of ideas.

In situations where I've seen no hatches of aquatics, but the trout were rising to *something,* I've taken the time to collect samples of what's drifing down in the surface film. On a windy day, the bag can contain as many as fifty species of flies.

During the evening when many of the insects fly forth with the cool breezes, one sees the swallows after them along with the bats and trout. Hundreds of insects. Anyone who tells me that under these conditions a specific

insect imitation is going to score better than a gray hackle or a small Wulff fly or a bivisible or a Swisher-Richards or even an Ovington is stretching my credulity.

But, if you want to let loose your creativity, tying an imitation of a land-bred insect is a challenge. To make a reasonable imitation it takes creativity that will have to burst the bonds of conventional fly tying and even most of the usual fly-tying materials.

I believe in the land-bred imitation school, if for no other reason that it will be fun making the creation. Catch fish? Of course it will—darn near any fly will catch fish at one time or another. If we can conjure up a situation and catch a fish on a one-of-a-kind type of fly and find reasonable justification for the idea that the trout took it for what it was supposed to represent, all well and good.

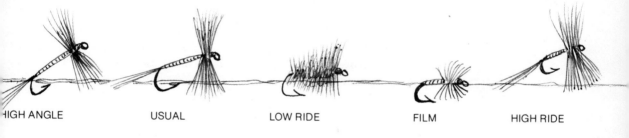

HIGH ANGLE        USUAL        LOW RIDE        FILM        HIGH RIDE

## Choice of Dry-Fly Size and Shape

I'm convinced that the size and shape of the dry fly is as much or more important than the actual pattern and colors. And I've got lots of records to prove the contention. I have touched on this subject in the section on fly tying and in fact detailed some tying hints in this respect.

Not just any old dry fly will do, even if it is a good standard pattern and one that is in the fish's demand, such as a fly that approximates the insects that are hatching at the moment you are on the stream. Sure, the conventional store-boughts will and do catch fish, no question; but I like to go 'em one step better. That's why fly tying is a must, in my opinion, if the dry-fly fisherman is to derive

USUAL        LONG        SHORT        **61**

the utmost in fishing satisfaction. It is very limiting to stick to the regulation fly.

I have arrived at a set of fly dimensions to fit certain types of water. I'd rather change a fly to suit the water than to suit the fish. In so doing, I'll catch him, just as long as the general coloration is somewhere close to what *he* sees.

My contention is that he must be able to see *any* fly, and mine, hopefully, will then appeal to him as looking somewhat like the steak and potatoes he seeks.

These dimensions fall into three basic categories. The first, of course, is the standard-size dry fly as illustrated here. That is the all-purpose one and sometimes the best. There are times, however, that a smaller pattern of the same fly will be more appealing since it will land with less fuss on the water and not be so big that it appears far different than the natural. This fly can be tied in two ways. If it is desired to have this fly float deep, that is, right in the surface film to be seen, then the fly is tied a size smaller than the conventional fly size. This naturally calls for a proportionately larger hook so that the weight ratio puts the fly where it belongs: right on the water, not above it with only the hackle points penetrating the surface. The alternative to this is to tie the smaller fly on a much larger hook. Either way. For example, suppose we want a light Cahill. The recommended size to approximate the hatch is a size 12 conventional fly. This fly usually is tied to ride high off the water or at least not sit on the film. So, we go to the fly-tying vise with a size 10 hook and tie the fly to the prescribed size 12 dimensions. Good on glassy water.

If, in another situation, we want this fly to ride high off the water, to float under bubbly, wavy, and rough water conditions, we tie the conventional size 12 fly on a 14 or even 16 hook. With less weight ratio, this fly will bounce on the water like a puffball and will be just the medicine for the fast runs, for quick casting, dropping, short drift and recast system used in fishing at, say, the top of a run where it is not desired to have the fly float for any distance.

One of my most potent Cahills is a size 12 tied on a size 18 hook!

Splitting hairs? Yes, and with good reason.

I can recall fishing a specific pool on the Esopus in late

May. Now, this water is broad, wide, deep, and at times quite fast, even in the big pools. Toward the head of this pool the surface is not rushing, but it is riddled with little current ripples and feed lanes. I've stood and watched the drifting duns riding on this water. A close look will find them with their bodies right in the film whereas in the slower, flat water they tend to ride higher, just on their legs. This observation begs for imitation.

The fish are rising to these duns—a little trout, medium-sized trout, and there's one big bruiser up there about an easy fifty-foot cast away that's just bulging the surface, hitting the insects that come to within a foot of him. The binoculars reveal that the insects are right down, flat on the surface. My conventional dry fly goes into the fray, once, twice, three times. Not a tumble.

One of the duns alights on my wrist. My conventional fly now in hand looks as if the two could be married, for my Cahills, even in conventional size, are closer than the standard dressings.

But the trout don't think so.

Now, we go forth with a size 14 fly on my 10 hook . . . and it would appear that the hook would be too large and that it might even scare the fish. But we keep on forgetting that trout have never heard of hooks. For all he knows, that hook might be a piece of grass. See, we have all these notions about scaring trout by the hook we insert in the fraud. They don't know from hooks!

This one goes right into the headwaters just a few feet above the big trout that's still filling his stomach.

Bingo! We're on!

Now, this might read like a manufactured situation and

appear somewhat fictitious. Don't you believe it! I've proven this bit so many times that I've forgotten the number. Yet the answer to catching that particular trout is really just that simple.

Now, let's look at the reverse situation. Some Cahills are bouncing out of bubbly water amid froth, surf, and a conglomeration of currents that present a kaleidoscopic situation. Best bet here is to abandon the conventional fly and especially the fly that sinks low to the film. We want a little guy to bounce and flip around on the surface and stay afloat. So, we tie a size 12 Cahill on a size 18 hook. We will not expect even this lightweight to float very far and, in fact, don't want it to, for we are going to tease the trout.

We'll cast that fly and don't care if it drops gently. We'll let it bounce a couple of times and quickly recast and recast to the identical spot on the water, right in between the naturals, and right where we see the trout rising. The extra casting and slapping of the water will not be noticed by the trout—it's all too muddled to show up the slapping leader. We'll use the roll-pickup cast rather than the conventional drag-through-the-water pickup. That fly will land on the water on every cast and remain there for, at most, two or three seconds.

On one of those drops, a trout hits, and the mere action of our prescribed pickup is enough to hook him. He didn't have a chance to reject it. We literally pulled him out of the water. In the case of a big fish, the technique is to have the spare line gripped very loosely in the hand. When the roll-pickup cast is used and a trout hits, the line is allowed to slip through the fingers without any holdback, until the fish goes under. Once hooked it is a matter of playing him out. Boy, what fun!

How many times have you tried to drift a dry fly and expected it to float down that water properly? No way . . . and even if it did, the trout would have time to reject it even if he did hit it. Casting and retrieving in this manner with a fly that is designed for the act is a moment in the dry-fly fisher's experience that's hard to beat.

It just goes to prove again that purism in fly fishing should be left in the ancient books to be read, absorbed, and then forgotten. When Halford and the others of our cult masters devised and developed the sport of dry-fly

fishing they did so as pioneers. Also, they were attempting to standardize fly tying and fishing methods to create a school concept.

We find this in all the arts. Music is no exception. The laws of harmony formulated and developed by Bach and learned by every beginner in harmony are rules not to be broken, yet look what Stravinski and the Beatles have done with harmony, beat, and prescribed phrasing.

Few dry-fly fishermen ever fish the way described above. They have been taught that the dry fly must float, drag free, on the surface. This is so in chalk streams in England and in a few streams in the United States, at certain times and under certain conditions. Yet the spider fly which is particularly effective on glassy water is the opposite of all this dogma. I have dealt with this lover in the section of this chapter titled Spiders. The spider shatters all purism and catches trout in a most exciting way.

And when they're hitting light—just bouncing up to a fly, not really wanting it, or deciding at the last split second to reject it—what do you do? Do you place that fly high off the water so they cannot really get a good look at it? No. The reason I believe they are rejecting it is because it doesn't look succulent enough. Put that fly right down in the film. Use a Cahill that's made with a generous fur body, well fluffed out.

## Quill Gordon

In 1950 in my first book, *How To Take Trout on Wet Flies and Nymphs,* I detailed the species specifications and identifications of the nymphs' and the Sens' imitations of this basic list of insects—mayflies and caddis and stone flies found during the cycle of the season. This was actually an extension of the great work of Preston Jennings and later, Art Flick, though my book dealt more heavily with the presentation technique. This was followed in 1969 by even more presentation techniques in my *Tactics on Trout.* This details, using many examples, the ways I've found successful for these hatches. Among the principal types of insects were the Quill Gordon, Hendrickson, March Brown, Light Cahill, and Giant Stone Fly.

The Hendrickson is a favorite fly. Basically an eastern

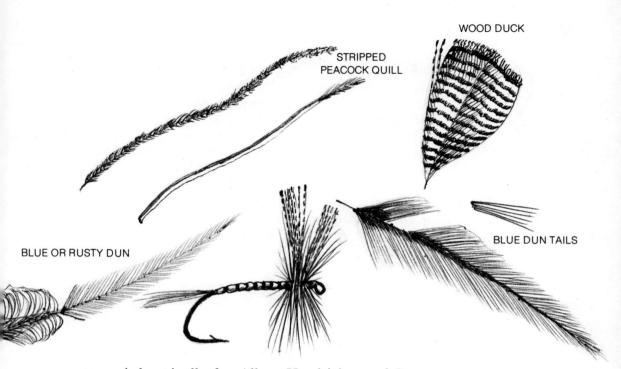

STRIPPED
PEACOCK QUILL

WOOD DUCK

BLUE DUN TAILS

BLUE OR RUSTY DUN

pattern tied orginally for Albert Hendrickson of Scarsdale, New York, it has won favor as a general nymph, wet-fly and dry-fly patterns, and is used on most streams including those of the Pacific Coast. The Quill Gordon was a product of Theodore Gordon, one of the first fly-tiers in the United States and a specialist at tying flies that were productive on eastern streams, particularly of the Catskills and Pennsylvania. The March Brown, basically an English import, is another favorite on the list, as is the Light Cahill, tied by Dan Cahill, a New York resident of the early 1900s. In this section I'd like to cover these insects as dry flies and their presentation.

In order to do this, it is important to know something about the insect they are tied to represent: the habits, habitat in the stream, manner of hatching, and the spinner, or adult stage. The trout know these patterns and we should too. Then we can go to work trying to make the best imitation possible.

For biological identification of the Quill Gordon, its order is Ephemeroptera; family, Heptageniidae; genus, *Iron*; species, *pleuralis* or *fradator*. Sometimes *epeorus* accompanies it, a very similar mayfly.

The size of the dun, that is, the subimago stage before the adult stage of the spinner, is body, ⅜ inch; wings, ⁷⁄₁₆, tails (two), ½ inch long. (Some of the mayflies have three

tails.) Coloration is medium gray with slight yellow cast, though some insects tend to be brownish and even slightly rust color. The legs are tan-gray, and the wings smokey blue-gray. The Blue Quill, Iron Blue Dun, and the Quill Gordon are apt imitations in hook sizes 12 and 14, though I prefer 16s, a bit overdressed so that they float better in the high, roily water of early spring.

If we are lucky on opening day in the East, which generally falls in early April, the water is cold and few, if any, insects are hatching, nor are there many land breds about. The water temperature is generally from thirty-eight degrees to forty-five degrees, which is not conducive to fly hatches unless a warm sun and a breeze that is not too chilly tends to warm the water surface. If the stream is very high with snow runoff, the hatches will likely be postponed. Lucky is the dry-fly fisherman who finds a hatch of these insects, unless an exceptionally warm spell prevails for at least a week before the opening date. When it happens, the nymphs of this insect (living as they do in the fastest parts of the rocky areas of the stream) take off from the bottom, drift for a few yards, and then hatch, usually in midstream. The best areas to fish are the slower sections just below the heads of pools or runs, or in the case of the shelving ripple, well out into the belly water away from the break in the current.

Since it is the first spring mayfly to offer any kind of a quantity hatch, it will be found to emerge at the warmest time of the day, that is, from noon to about three o'clock. If the water is clear, it is best to use as fine a leader as possible, since the trout are not yet in the habit of making rash rises to floating insects. They can be easily put down from the feeding spree if the casts are sloppy and leaders are too noticeable.

On the other hand, they are hungry and will follow the nymphs to the surface and feed on the duns voraciously if conditions warrant.

The spinner or adult stage of this insect occurs when the dun fully hatches on the surface, flies around for a few hours, and then settles into the willows and on the grasses along the stream's edges. There the insect sheds its dun skin and becomes a fleeting, thinner insect with mother-of-pearl, transparent wings and a dark gray, almost black, body. The egg sac is the important item here, as the adult state of the mayfly contains little or no food value. The trout are really after the egg sac which is attached to the abdomen of the female just ahead of the long tails. The Lady Beaverkill, while originally made as an imitation of the female gray caddis, is also a very good fly, tied in the dry style as a spinner imitation of the Quill Gordon. I should also include here my version of this spinner as well as my own pet dressing for the dun of the species.

In the afternoon of the next day, the spinner usually returns to the stream, dancing and mating in the air just above the water surface, and generally near the head of a pool or run. When the midair mating is done, the eggs quickly develop, and the female dips down to the water surface to let the passing water tick them off from her. After a few minutes she is dead or dying, floating on the surface, wings straight out from her body in spent wing form.

Dry-fly time? You bet. But, again, take care in casting lest you put the finicky big trout off their feed.

Most of us can remember (even those of us with a scant amount of visual acumen) having seen these small gray flies during the early part of the season. Many years ago, while fishing the upper reaches of the Logan River in Utah, I noted that this fly was predominant even during hatches of other mayflies. The other flies seen then were probably Hendricksons, which often hatch early, thereby overlapping with this hatch. I've had the same experience on Ten Mile Creek in Putnam County, New York, where I've fished the opening days of many seasons with Don Leyden and Ed Sens and a host of other fly-fishermen from the canyons of the city.

You'll see the early arriving phoebes darting out from the still unleaved branches of the alders and among the fuzzing pussy-willow pods along the stream. They like these early mayflies as much as the trout do.

The Quill Gordon was and still is a favored imitation fished by countless anglers on the Catskill streams such as the Esopus, Beaverkill, Willowemoc, and Neversink. Visit the Folkert Brothers Store in Phoenicia during the first two weeks of the year and their fly trays will be almost empty of them. Harry Darbee on the Beaverkill raises his own blue dun roosters, a special strain of chicken he's developed over many years. In most cases he does not kill the rooster to take the neck skin, since the feathers are so valuable. He plucks them out instead, and if you visit his yard at this time of the year, you'll see some very funny-looking roosters stalking around.

This little innocuous fly is most difficult to see, especially on an early spring day if the sky is gray and overcast. Add to this the usual drabness of the water due to snow runoff and roily conditions, and the following of the fly on the water is an eyestrainer. Edward R. Hewitt, developer of the bivisible, no-wing fly, included in his types the gray bivisible, that is, an all-hackle fly of gray color but fronted by a few turns of white to catch what light there might be on the river. The Iron Blue Dun is another standard especially for the eastern streams.

My own patterns for the Quill Gordon and similar little gray mayflies (and also the gray caddis that hatches with it) are included here just in case you want to try a variation from the norm.

FEMALE QUILL GORDON (Lady Beaverkill is the standard here)
*Hook size:* Short shank #14–#16
*Tails:* Sparse, sandy, and long
*Egg sac:* One turn of thin yellow or off-yellow chenille
*Body:* Gray and white (alternated) silk wound to hackle
*Wings:* One wisp of white calf hair or skunk
*Hackle:* Blend of gray and dirty yellow–brown (dyed)
*Head:* Black

MALE QUILL GORDON
*Hook size:* Short shank #14–#16
*Tails:* Sparse; sandy gray; long
*Body:* Gray and white (alternated) silk wound to hackle
*Wings:* Wisp of short white calf
*Hackle:* Blend of dark gray and light brown

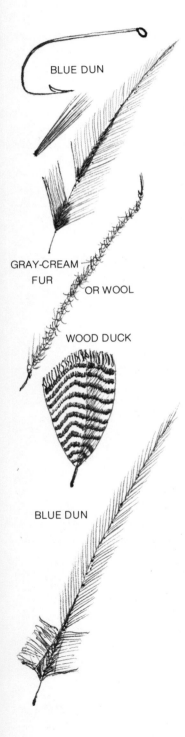

BLUE DUN

GRAY-CREAM
FUR
OR WOOL

WOOD DUCK

BLUE DUN

SPINNER QUILL GORDON
*Hook size:* #16
*Tails:* Sparse; sandy gray
*Body:* Black and gray (alternated) silk wound to hackle
*Wings:* Sparse wisp of long white calf
*Hackle:* Blend of black and sandy brown

When the caddis hatch is on, try the same colors and hook size, but make the wings out of gray mallard duck quill, slanted backwards. One further refinement is in the type of fly. For ultra-fast water, I like the fly to sink into the film rather than ride high and possibly go unnoticed. Use shorter, softer, wet-fly type hackle. Since this fly hatches in the fast-moving water, this dressing is recommended. For the slick and glassier stretches, use a fly that rides higher, unless the water is cloudy or murky.

## The Hendrickson

While hatches of the Quill Gordon are generally light and sporadic, the Hendricksons have the tendency to hatch all at once and quite often in droves. When they combine with a big hatch of brown caddis, both trout and angler have a real time of it—the trout filling their gullets and the angler lucky if he hooks one fish, due to the fish's choice of nailing the real thing as it is hatching or fluttering on the surface.

The water has to warm up quite a bit in order to have this hatch. The temperature must be close to fifty degrees for at least a week to permit hatching. Like the Quill Gordon, the Hendrickson begins to be seen in the late morning and continues into the afternoon unless a cold wind and heavy overcast sky discourage them.

The nymph of this fly does not live in the fastest water areas such as those favored by the Quill Gordon. Unless a hatch has taken place well upstream, the Hendrickson will be seen popping up in the center or even lower section of a

long pool or section of fairly flat water. The nymph takes its time, drifting sometimes for a quarter of a mile from its gravelly underwater residence before becoming magnetized by the surface film. There it struggles valiantly and takes more time than the Quill Gordon to shed its nymphal shuck and finally take to the air. The watchful angler can see the Hendrickson nymphs drifting by him in the water and so can just about pin the watch down as to the time of the hatch. Up until that time, trout will be seen flashing underwater and then finally taking the hatching insects from the film. Then comes dry-fly time de luxe. Switch to the floater now.

I can recall many, many hatches where I've had the opportunity to hook and release as many as twenty trout within the confines of an hour and return home with many mangled dry flies. Given these conditions, the dry-fly angler really puts all other methods to shame if the aim of fishing is to hook trout. It was during one Hendrickson hatch of large magnitude and success that I decided to switch to the barbless hook, since it made it easier to either shake the trout loose after the initial battle or to return them unharmed from the net to the water.

Biologically speaking, the order of this mayfly is Ephemeroptera; family, Ephemerellidae; genus, *Ephemerella*; species, *invaria, subvaria*, and *rotunda* (often appearing together). The body of the dun is $\frac{5}{16}$ to $\frac{3}{8}$ inch, tails (three) $\frac{3}{8}$ to $\frac{7}{16}$ inch. Dun body color is medium ruddy brown with gray-tan legs. Wings: iron gray; tails: tan gray.

The most successful pattern is the Hendrickson, but the Hewitt light-tan bivisible is a good substitute as is the Brown Quill, an old English pattern and the Whirling Brown Dun, also popular in Europe. The hook size in legitimate size tying would be 12 or 14, though I sometimes like to dress a 16 hook with a size 14 fly and hackle so that the fly will float for a longer distance. While this insect is seen in the fast water due to an upstream hatch, it generally hatches in quieter water especially along the stream edges and tantalizingly near the underhanging foliage, offering, in high water, a tough casting proposition.

At the lower reaches of a long pool, where the water flattens out in runs between the rocks and gravel and where the depth is only about knee deep, you'll find these insects hatching in droves and making superlong drifts. Careful casting and approaching them with ultralong casts will bring results. Wading up to these areas too closely will likely put them down. It is best to work this kind of water with a long cast high above their location and then allow the long leader to drift the fly over them as unobtrusively as possible.

As to pattern, Theodore Gordon tied this one for Albert Hendrickson, and it has yet to be topped. I have developed an equally good, though hardly celebrated, pattern for the dun and also the spinner which I include here for those who like to ad-lib.

Here again, when the hatch is on or even about to start, the early spring anglers with their streamers and bucktails and yes, even my friends who like their nymphing, will be outshown by the casting of a well-tied Hendrickson pattern of floater. When a great many of the insects are on the water, even the fresh hatchery trout will devour them. Anyone who looks down their finicky noses at hatchery trout will change their minds when they see those trout gobble up these mayflies and on occasion, take the artificial version. Again, the barbless hook comes in handy here, and the anglers seeing your constant returning of trout back to their element, will ask to see what you are using. You'll likely pick up some converts.

I've seen this insect or its equivalent (there are some 500 mayfly species in the United States) on rivers such as the Lower Kings River in California, a small version of it on Hot Creek in the Sierras, and in countless Rocky Mountain streams from New Mexico to northern Idaho and Montana. In the East, there are specific hatches on the Ausable in New York in the last week of May and on the La Molle in upper Vermont in June, likewise on the Allagash in upper Maine in late June. The Catskills and lower New England states generally find this fly hatching from late April through May.

I can recall fishing New York's Ausable and witnessing a Hendrickson hatch that was as momentous as the famed Green Drake hatch of that river. The insects rose and floated for many yards in a mass downstream drift. The trout went crazy. Even the big ones were bouncing around the surface. Two nights later when the spinners of this hatch were above the water, I experienced one of the best spinner hatches of my life. Taking trout on my pattern of the Hendrickson spinner was a delight, and I was glad that I'd taken the time and interest to develop the pattern. That some other fly might have done as well is merely an uninteresting conjecture.

Here are some of my patterns for this fly in the dun and spinner states.

Note: On many of the eastern streams especially, a darker phase of the Hendrickson fly is seen in company with *invaria*. This is the Dark Hendrickson species: *cupida*. It is not to be confused with the later hatch of the larger insect to follow it: the March Brown and its lighter contemporary, the Gray Fox.

The first use of the spider fly can be experienced during this hatch when there are sufficient flies on the water and action to them. Given fairly smooth water ruffled a bit by puffy breezes, the spider tied on a size 16 short, turned-up eye hook, using light brown hackles, will offer good action during this hatch and also during the return spinner flight at twilight.

FEMALE HENDRICKSON (Lady Beaverkill is a fair representation)
*Hook size:* #14; medium long
*Tails:* Wood duck or mallard flank feather fibers; sparse
*Egg sac:* Thin yellow chenille; sparse
*Body:* Gray wool crossed by fine gold wire
*Wings:* Wisp of light tan calf or dirty squirrel tail; short
*Hackle:* Blend of gray and sand colored; soft hackles so body rests on water

MALE HENDRICKSON
*Hook size:* #14; medium long
*Tails:* Tan-gray hackle points; stripped
*Body:* Gray thread, cotton, crossed with brown thread
*Wings:* Wisp of wood duck flank feather or dirty mallard flank
*Hackle:* Blend of dark gray and light brown

SPINNER HENDRICKSON
*Hook size:* #14; medium long
*Tails:* Dark brown stripped quill

*Body:* Black and brown cotton thread
*Wings:* Wisp of light brown calf very thin and short
*Hackle:* Dark brown

## March Brown

A fly closely resembling the March Brown was an import from England at the turn of the century. Or perhaps
we should say that the American March Brown closely
resembles the original pattern tied in England a long time
ago. Anyhow, it is a good fly—a good general fly that in
all its forms, nymph, wet, and dry, seems to take trout.
The nearest mayfly insect in this resemblance is the
species, *vicarium*; genus, *Stenonema*; family, Heptageniidae; and order, of course, Ephemeroptera. It resides as a
nymph in the same type of water where the Quill Gordon
is found: the rocky and fast sections of the stream where it
clings to the rocks until ready to hatch.

The March Brown dun and its lighter phase the Gray
Fox (species, *fuscum*) have one easily spotted identification not found in many of the other mayflies. These two
slant their wings back at a forty-five degree angle as op-
posed to almost upright wings in other species. The dun of
the March Brown has rust-brown tails, alternate bands of
cream and rust brown on the abdomen, with broad wings
colored light gray mottled with black, giving off an
overall, light tan-olive cast that is really difficult to imitate
in feathers. It is a medium-size mayfly, being $\frac{9}{16}$ of an inch
long of body, with $\frac{5}{8}$ inch wings. Like the Quill Gordon, it
has two tails $\frac{1}{2}$ inch long.

Following along after the first big hatches of Hendricksons, the March Browns really put us into the true
dry-fly fishing to rising and drifting mayflies. They usually hatch in large numbers, with the hatch beginning at
the head of a pool. Starting with a few insects at a time,
the amount increases until the full pool is rippling with
fluttering insects and nearly always many trout dimpling
and even jumping well out to grab the fluttering ones. The
March Brown does not pop out of the water once the
nymph skin is shucked. It tends to ride for quite a spell on
the water, trying out its tails and flexing its wings. I've

seen them drift down through a pool and if not gobbled up by a trout or minnow, they will sally down the tail of the pool, over the riffs and then, perhaps, take off for a near-by bush.

The water temperature is now at or above fifty degrees, especially during the midday, and this hatch, starting as it might at 10 o'clock in the morning, can extend to about three o'clock, when it dwindles, giving us quite a few hours of excellent midday angling. If during this time there are puffs or stiff bursts of wind, these insects will be blown into bunches on the water, driving the trout and other fish into a fantastic feeding orgy. It takes little talent to hook a dozen trout in a few moments during such a time as this.

But there are times, even when a few of these insects are floating down, that expert and careful casting is needed. Also, when the water is glassy, the trout can, because of the midday glare, become very finicky risers. An artificial drifted among the naturals will likely score if, like the real thing, there is no leader drag. Given a sudden breeze, however, the Neversink Skater or a brown-colored spider fly will be as good or better than the standard pattern.

The March Brown hatches occur in central New York and Pennsylvania and in Montana and Oregon from May 15th to June 15th; later, however, in the more northern streams. In Montana, the March Brown is often accompanied by the Brown Caddis and the little brown stone fly, which makes identification of the naturals a bit difficult for the average spotter. In any case, the March Brown fly tied as standard or, if you like to experiment, my pattern, will be the setup for some action.

For those who fish the Beaverkill, Esopus, Willowemoc, and Neversink in the Catskills and the Ausable in northern Adirondack country and, for that matter, the streams of southern New England and Pennsylvania, the March Brown hatch is every bit as important as the Green Drake. By now, even the hatchery trout are well schooled in the taking of floating and hatching flies and offer every bit as much sport as any of the natural-bred trout or last year's holdovers.

My dressing for the March Brown starts with a size 12, long shank, lightweight hook. The tails are golden pheasant crest, similar to that used on the Royal Coachman.

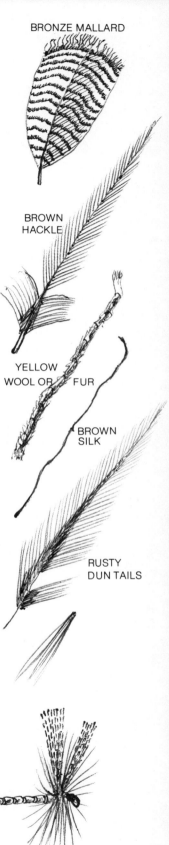

BRONZE MALLARD

BROWN HACKLE

YELLOW WOOL OR FUR

BROWN SILK

RUSTY DUN TAILS

For the body of this fly, I like wool, even if it makes the fly a bit heavy. I mix rust and light tan together and band the body with fine gold wire, picking out the hairs to make the body buggy looking. I tie no wings, not even white wisps, since this fly is cast during the daytime. Rather, I wind on the mottled fibers from a hen pheasant or mallard breast feather or even grouse mottled feather, if I have been lucky in my fall hunting the year before. Two turns is enough. Then I add variant hackle that includes brown and even almost black-brown fibers. A simple fly to tie, it appears bunchy on the water or buggy looking and seems to work well.

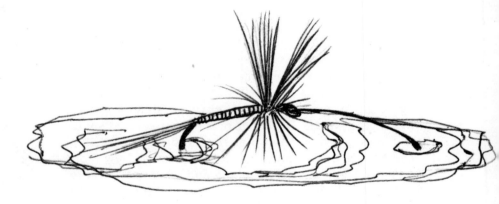

For the spinner version, I darken all the colors and for the body, use only black and brown cotton thread for the abdomen and eliminate the grouse feathers in the hackle. It's a good fly in the evening when the March Brown spinners are over the water. Oh, yes, the egg sac: a wisp of yellow chenille at the base of the tail just ahead of the bend of the hook.

I use this spinner fly imitation quite often during the entire season as a fish finder. There are times even during the major hatches when there is not a single insect on the water. I try to create a hatch with this fly over a given run or riffle, repeating the casts over and over again. I usually get a rise even if it is only from a chub. But there have been times when I've tempted lunkers out of seemingly impossible spots with such technique. This fly works well even when the Cahills are hatching.

## Green Drake

Come with me to New York's Adirondack Mountains, and fish with me on the famed Ausable during the first two weeks in June when the Green Drake is scheduled. Give or take a few days and you'll really hit into the peak of dry-fly fishing on this momentous river. True, there are countless rivers all over the map that have this hatch, from Montana (and even the streams of Oregon have a similar mayfly) and, of course, all through the East and in Pennsylvania waters such as the Paradise Creek and the slower, almost English, chalk stream types of which Charlie Fox and his coterie write with eloquence.

The Green Drake nymph is a mud dweller; it is quite large for a mayfly nymph and burrows in the shallow waters where the mud collects. You'll never see them in the fast water or at the head of a pool unless of course they have hatched above and have been blown into the pool to drift down over the waterfalls and rushes.

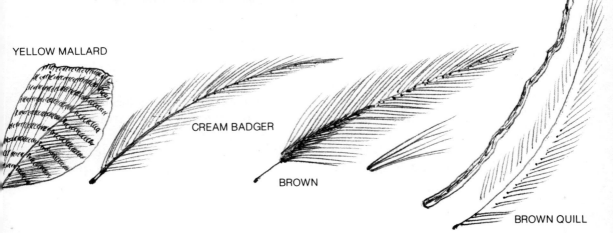

YELLOW MALLARD

CREAM BADGER

BROWN

RAFFIA

BROWN QUILL

One advantage during this hatch is that it happens usually in midday when the insects crawl out of the water at the stream edge or on to a rock or along the edges of the stream in the gravel and sand. At this time of the year most of the mayfly and caddis hatches come off at twilight or early evening when the pool has cooled off and the harsh sun has departed behind the hills. This leaves the hatch all to itself. There is no confusion. When enough of these big flies are on the water, the trout really come out of hiding and take part in a feast that they must look forward to all year long. They don't go wild during the hatch. They don't have to. They take up a position along or under a current split or where the current tends to funnel the floating debris down the stretch. Those trout may have come out from an undercut bank fifty feet away, moved up from the underlip of a shelving riffle, or dropped down from the aerated and cool waters under the lip of the rapids that forms the pool in which they reside.

The duns float down in large formations much like a sailboat race-week convention. Here they come . . . there's two of them isolated from the rest. One disappears with not so much as a trace. There goes the other one. Who got them? Minnow or big brown? You can't tell unless the light is right and you can see into the water.

You cast your dry fly to the edge of the stream of insects and it lands with some water disturbance. *Bingo*! That commotion drew the eyes of the trout right to your fly. Try again. Same result. One would think that it would be proper to drift that fly as silently and drag-free as the real insects, but it is seldom necessary to do this. Those trout are alert to what's floating over them in their forms of beefsteak, and since no other flies are about, they know what's what. All you have to do is to plop your fly in among them, or as mentioned, preferably to the side of the drifting clusters of insects and you'll hit pay dirt.

One of the best hatches to select when you want to impress someone with your prowess with the dry fly, particularly for a beginner, is the Green Drake. The flies are big and even if the casting is not perfected, he'll take trout and that's the main point.

This is not to say that it is *always* that easy. After the hatch has been going on for a few minutes and the fish have gotten over their first burst of feeding, they begin to settle down a bit and become very touchy. They also are more prone to flight at the landing of your line on the water. You'll likely get light hits from then on. If the hatch is not a full one, the trout will not be so rash.

During this hatch, when things begin to calm down in the pool, I usually go ashore and walk quickly downstream, or even get into the car and drive down to a pool a half mile below. If there has not been a hatch there, the floating duns will be there shortly, and you'll be able to repeat what went on up above. During this hatch it is most important to be in the right place at the right time. If you are not in the right place, the duns can drift down over the stuffed trout, and you'll wonder if there is a fish in the river.

Strangely enough, the dun of the Green Drake is not really green, and I've seen Hendricksons of a much earlier hatch more green or even olive in color. They vary from stream to stream, of course, and that is one reason why I have never been a nut on trying to duplicate the subtle differences of insect color in the dry fly, preferring to try and approximate the illusion they give to the trout as seen from under the water surface. I still maintain that that vague impression is important, a factor that certainly was of great importance in the development of the hackleless fly as presented by Swisher-Richards. I've used the hackleless fly on the Green Drake hatch and not found it wanting. However, I caught fish on those trips with almost any color of fly, just so long as it looked from underneath the surface like a big mayfly. Try my hackleless fan wing.

If you can, work in a suggestion of orange and tan with a turn or two of olive hackle . . . same with the body. The Green Drake pattern I show here is my compromise pattern which I've found to be the most reliable. If this doesn't produce, I quickly switch to one of my variants and usually save the day with them.

After the Green Drake on some waters, particularly streams that have an abundance of area that is muddy, there are several other big-size mayflies that hatch. One is a bright white-yellow, and the old English Yellow Sally in the fan wing is perfect medicine.

The adult, or spinner of the Green Drake, is called the

Coffin Fly, and many a trout has been taken on this imitation—a standard fly, by the way, for some fifty years that I can recall.

This is a fly tied with black-and-white tails, white or cream-white body, black-and-white hackles and white or light gray mallard flank feather wings. Many patterns call for mere black or rust-black hackle-point wings. The big Wulff dry flies of black, gray, or gray-tan will also work well, though they are dressed much too heavily and thickly.

Again, in this case, I prefer the variant and don't forget the egg sac. That's the most important part.

The spinners begin to appear at the end of twilight and into the evening. As the light begins to quit, tie on a big Hewitt spiderlike bivisible with the wisps of white at the front, and you'll be able to at least see what's going on near your fly.

←EGG SAC

Quite often the spinners will cause more of a ruckus than the duns did, unless, of course, the trout are still logy from the debauchery of the afternoon when a generous flotilla of Green Drake duns drifted down the pike.

Here are some of my patterns to tie up and use at your will.

This spinner is one of the most popular with flytiers. Many of the old-time flies have been concocted to imitate the Green Drake spinner insect. Over the years I've also played with the creative urge and have been able to come up with some good imitations; that is, flies that, on the water, appear to closely resemble the insect. Not that they took trout any better than any light-phase fly with long hackles or certainly the spider. Try these below, for kicks anyway. They just might catch fish!

A darker version of this fly can employ tail and wings of silver fox tail fibers, black-and-white tying silk body, segmented and blended black and grizzled hackle. Grizzled hackle point wings can also be used, but make them short to avoid wind resistance.

*Hook size:* #12, long shank, turned-up eye
*Tying thread:* White silk
*Tails:* Few wisps of white tipped squirrel tail fibers
*Body:* Few wisps of squirrel tail fibers rolled first and then tied in to show segmentation of insect body; short body

*Substitute body:* Alternated black-and-tan cotton thread, lacquered

*Wings:* White tipped squirrel tail, fanned out, not separated in conventional wing design

*Hackle:* Grizzled, generous and long

*Egg sac:* Include this on all patterns; yellowish tan floss or yarn as a bump just ahead of the hook (see illustrations)


## Cahills: Light and Dark

Now, this is the hatch that is most popular, particularly in the East. Coming as it does in June and often extending into July, depending on the temperature belt, this fly offers the longest sessions on the stream. Cahills generally don't start to hatch until the shadows begin to lengthen on the stream and the water cools a bit. In streams that tend to warm up at this season, particularly if the water levels are down, these flies are usually twilight hatchers, coming out about an hour before dusk and extending until well after the last gold light has left the pool's reflections. The no-see-ums and mosquitoes join in the fun to harass the angler. Then too, from the angling point of view, there are countless other very small flies, particularly midges, that appear on the scene to cause conflicts of interest among the feeding trout.

The Cahill is a small insect, with the body only a half inch long of cream-buff color, darker in the darker Cahill phase. The wings are cream or a dusty, yellowish, milky coloration, and the legs light and slightly mottled tan. The standard light (or dark) Cahill, cream bivisible, Red Fox, Red Quill, and Ginger Quill are apt imitations that work well during these hatches. Also a light tan spider should be included and the Hewitt-type tan bivisible.

When the hatch starts, the trout usually seem to be quiet about their feeding. I've stood by, holding back my casting to watch the little duns float down a long slick glide. With the eyes focused on a single fly, it can be seen to disappear without even the slightest ring or surface commotion. They can be watched disappearing like this, and one wonders just what kind of underwater critter is at work. It could be a simple little chub, but there again, a

WOOD DUCK

LIGHT GINGER

LIGHT CREAM    FUR OR WOOL

LIGHT GINGER
TAIL

monster brown could be underneath. The rainbows usually make quite a fuss, but quite often the brown will merely suck in the insect by its legs. One explanation given me by Art Flick explains that this action is the result of the browns resting in the current with their noses just under the surface. They usually do this because they are feeding on midges, and when a larger fly comes along, they treat it the same way—merely suck it in without any celebration.

Anyhow, the drama of the evening rise is at its peak during this hatch, especially when the spinners of these and other insects are dancing above the water and dipping down to the surface to deposit their eggs. One would think that almost any pattern would suffice, and sometimes this is the case. But I'd hate to admit the number of such evenings when I've switched from fly to fly to absolutely no avail in the face of browns as long as your arm feeding right in front of me in a most obvious abandonment of all caution.

Biologically, the Light Cahill is of the order, Ephemeroptera; family, Heptageniidae; genus, *Stenonema* —which, so far, is similar to the March Brown and Gray Fox. Species is *ithiaca canadens*.

I have never tried to improve on the standard Cahill patterns or those mentioned above. They have been good enough for me.

The Cahills hatch at a beautiful time of the trout season, and it is good to be around on a long and gentle evening when the host of fishermen have left the stream for their favorite bass waters. Strangely enough, this best part of the season finds fewer anglers about, especially the spinning crowd and the live baiters. You have the stream virtually to yourself.

It's long leader time—spare the sloppy cast—and try for that drag-free drift.

And, of course, there are countless other mayflies in the cycle of the season. Next in line are the Little Marryat and Pale Evening Dun and a host of similar insects which really need not be imitated exactly due to the confusion of insects on any given evening, plus so many kinds of spinners. And we haven't even mentioned the numerous caddises and stone flies, much less the great numbers of landbred insects, especially millers and flying ants. It just gets too complicated. Fish a small dry carefully and change patterns constantly until you are lucky. That's the best advice.

The drama chaos usually calls for a fly smaller than the average seen on the water, handled most deftly. From here on in it is luck, regardless of what some experts preach.

The Brown Drake, or Leadwing Coachman, is another fly that hatches in the middle or late season and does so, strangely enough, in the bright light of day. Use any dark fly for him. The trout are either too finicky and will spot your fraud quickly or, conversely, they'll grab your fly merely because they are hungry.

The illustrated patterns can be tied in wet-fly style by slanting the wings backward and using soft and sparse hackles.

## Wet Flies, Nymphs, and Streamer Flies

Using small, wet trout flies is as old or older than dry-fly fishing. At first, these flies were skittered one, two, or even three to a leader on the surface of the water, were allowed to submerge, and were generally used in a kind of chuck-and-chance-it attitude. They looked like drowned insects or in some cases, emerging nymphs, and according to the way they were manipulated, they caught fish.

Wet flies, generally similar to the standard dry-fly patterns in the imitation school of the more drab feather and fur combinations, require as much art in their design, tying, and fishing as dry flies and are a delight to cast. There are pretty patterns in some older classic books that were, I imagine, designed more for their beauty than they were for actual insect imitation. These too caught trout and still catch them if you can duplicate the patterns and find the exotic feathers to form them. But I maintain that they are not necessary. Actually, when you strip all the voodoo and mystery away from successful wet-fly fishing, as I have attempted to do in my former books such as *Tactics on Trout, How To Take Trout on Wet Flies and Nymphs,* and *Freshwater Fishing,* you can do very well with some ten or twelve patterns in sizes 8 to 20. The technique of fishing them is basic and limited to a few tactics that can and do catch trout consistently.

Before detailing these flies and how to fish them, I wish to remind you that good balanced tackle is as important here as it is in dry-fly fishing and that the art of wet-fly fishing is every bit as special and spectacular as is dry-fly fishing. It is not a step *down* as some purists of the earlier

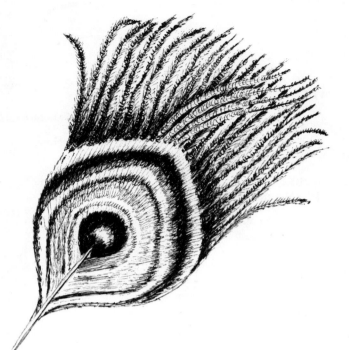

days would have your believe, despite the fact that their books have become classics.

As I detail in chapter 6, you must know how to read the stream for action in the feed lanes. You must know the currents, the trout habits, and how to wade the stream properly. May sound academic, but it's true.

But you learn all this as you go along and the wet fly is a perfect method of learning.

Listed in the following table are the patterns I consider the most versatile and the ones I use when I go fishing.

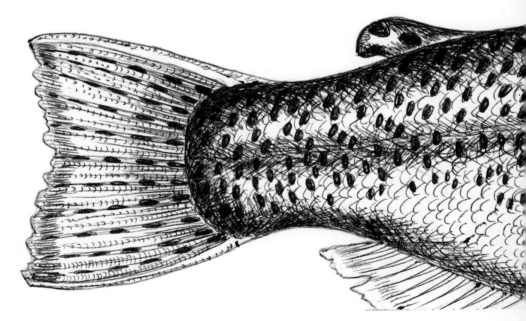

# WET-FLY PATTERNS

| Name | Hook | Tail | Body | Wings | Underhackle |
|------|------|------|------|-------|-------------|
| Black Quill | 16 | Black fibers | Black quill, white rib | Dark mallard | None |
| Blue Quill | 16 | Blue fibers | Blue yarn, white thread | Gray mallard | None |
| Quill Gordon | 14 | Gray fibers | Gray wool, black thread | Wood duck | None |
| Hendrickson | 14 | Brown fibers | Olive wool, gold wire | Brown wood duck | None |
| March Brown | 12 | Brown fibers | Brown wool, gold wire | Turkey | None |
| Gray Fox | 12 | Tan fibers | Gray wool, silver rib | Turkey | None |
| Leadwing Coachman | 14 | Brown fibers | Peacock | Gray mallard | None |
| Royal Coachman | 12 | Golden Pheasant | Peacock and red floss | White mallard | Brown |
| Green Drake | 12 | Brown fibers | Olive fur, yellow thread | White hackle tip | None |
| Yellow May | 12 | Tan fibers | Yellow yarn, white thread | Yellow hackle tip | None |
| Green Caddis | 14 | Black fibers | Olive green wool | Short, black hackle points | None |
| Gray Caddis | 14 | Brown fibers | Gray wool | Short, black hackle points | None |
| Little Stone Fly | 14 | Brown fibers | Brown-and-black fur, brown thread | Wing pads, cut turkey | Brown |
| Giant Stone Fly | 12 | Brown fibers | Brown fur, black yarn | Cut turkey | Brown |
| Whatsits | 12 | Gray fibers | Gray fur pulled out | Long black-and-white hackle all around | None |

In actual wet-fly, nymph, and streamer bucktail fishing, there are standard approaches to a given stretch of water. The most common is the downstream cast. This is done usually above a break in the stream such as a large rock or a shelving riffle or below a falls where the water begins to flatten out. Stream edges are other hot spots to fish, especially in under an undercut bank or in and around shoreline snags.

The downstream cast is also made with a lot of slack line in the air on cast. When the fly is about to alight on the water, the rod is pulled back hard, and the fly alights right in front of you to drift down into the selected run. This slack line fishing is tricky. You have to keep your eye on the line and watch it closely for a sudden movement indicating a strike. When the line is well downstream and the slack has been absorbed, it is alternately given short twitches and jerks to give life to it.

The across-and-downstream drift is another standard approach. The fly is cast across stream, sometimes slightly upstream, and the fly is allowed to sink on a slack line until it reaches the hot spot to be fished. It is then allowed to drift as if dead and twitched as in the downstream cast to imitate a rising nymph.

CURRENT → DRIFT

The third alternative is to cast the wet fly almost directly upstream, preferably just above a rock or snag. The fly will sink with the current, swimming by the snag in a long run. The same routine is followed as in the casts listed above as the fly is fished out to the limit.

In all cases, the fly should be fished back to the angler and allowed to wallow in the water all the way back to the rod tip.

In the early season, when there is not much insect activity on or near the surface, the wet fly should be fished as deep down as possible. This is accomplished by weighting the fly or weighting the leader or both. You have to dredge the bottom of a deep run or pool to fish the early season, unless there are signs of action on the surface such as feeding fish or rising and hatching insects.

Surface fishing with the wet fly, working the flies dead drift in the current or skittering the flies right on the surface film, can be the most effective method, especially where the water is less than three feet deep. Even the six-inch shallows will find feeding fish that will succumb to this method. The cast is made either up, up and across, or down and across, and the rod is held high with a fairly short line. The flies are literally dappled or lifted over the pockets. Sometimes even the roll cast can be added to flip the flies in any desired direction. The cast can be partially retrieved, and the flies roll cast right back to where they came from. This action is especially good in the evening when there are lots of insects on the water either floating dead or actually hatching on the surface. When there is a good wind on the stream, especially during the summer, there are a lot of land-bred insects that are blown in from the trees and nearby fields. The wet fly, even though it is not designed specifically to imitate the land-bred insect, will look buggy if given the proper action, and the trout will mistake it for the real thing.

As far as specific patterns are concerned, I have found that when there is not any action of hatching insects that the brighter attraction patterns such as the Royal Coachman, Silver Doctor, or almost any design that has a white wing will bring action. If there is a specific hatch of insects going on and the trout are concentrating on them, then a match of the hatch is required. Here the Iron Blue Dun, the Quill Gordon, the Hendrickson, the March Brown, the Green Drake, and the Yellow May come into being and can be most effective. This is not to throw out all other patterns, but over the years, I have come to the conclusion that it is better to spend the time fishing and learning presentation than to spend too much time in changing patterns.

ROYAL COACHMAN (WET)

## Nymphs

Nymphs and wet flies are closely related. They both tend to accomplish the same feat, that of fooling the trout into thinking that what he sees is a goodie he is feeding on or buggy looking. Many of the rules of wet-fly fishing apply to nymph fishing: In the early spring, when the water is cold and deep and no surface hatching action is evident, dredge the bottom. During the hatch, fish the surface film to imitate the hatching flies. The fine art of matching the hatch that is followed in dry-fly fishing is applicable here. There are nymph patterns that have been developed to imitate specific insect hatches of the mayflies and caddis flies. Those I have developed are shown here together with details on how to tie them. They are the underwater counterparts of the dry flies in the preceding chapter and should be used as such. True, almost any of them fished in a general way might catch a trout, but when the specific hatch is on and the trout are being horrifyingly selective, they will bring the results.

The same general casting and retrieving techniques as outlined for wet-fly fishing apply equally with the nymph: up and across and down, across and down, downstream drift, and swing in a fanned-out direction as shown in the wet-fly diagrams.

Academically, the nymph is the aquatic form of the dun and spinner of the mayfly. The caddis larva is considered a nymph in fishing terms. It is also aquatic and hatches on the water surface. Other water-bred insects such as the stone fly, fish fly, alder fly, and countless other forms offer food for the trout, and these can be well imitated by the nymph fished either in a dead drift natural state, as the insect would be carried in the current, or in short flashy jerks to copy its swimming and darting motions in the water.

In the first two chapters, I have attempted to describe just what happens on the trout stream, and I believe a thorough study of those pages followed by the right nymphs plus good presentation will provide the reader with enough information to have him go forth to the stream with confidence and catch a limit of trout. Anything more said here would duplicate what is in those two chapters.

BLACK QUILL

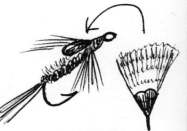

QUILL GORDON

HENDRICKSON

LEADWING COACHMAN

STONE FLY

ALL-ROUND

## NYMPH PATTERNS

| Name | Hook | Tail | Body | Wing Pads | Underhackle |
|------|------|------|------|-----------|-------------|
| Black Quill | 14/16 | Black fibers | Black yarn, white thread | Brown mallard | Black |
| Blue Quill | 14/16 | Black fibers | Purple wool, gold rib | Brown mallard | Black |
| Gray Quill (Quill Gordon) | 14/16 | Black fibers | Gray wool | Brown mallard | Gray |
| Hendrickson | 14/12 | Brown fibers | Olive wool, gold rib | Brown mallard | Brown and green |
| March Brown | 14/12 | Brown fibers | Tan wool, yellow rib | Brown mallard | Mixed brown and gray |
| Leadwing Coachman | 12/14 | Brown fibers | Peacock | Brown | Brown |
| Green Drake | 12 | Brown fibers | Tan-yellow wool, gold rib | Brown mallard | Yellow and gray |
| Stone Fly (med.) | 12/10 | Brown fibers | Brown-and-black yarn | Brown mallard | Mottled brown |

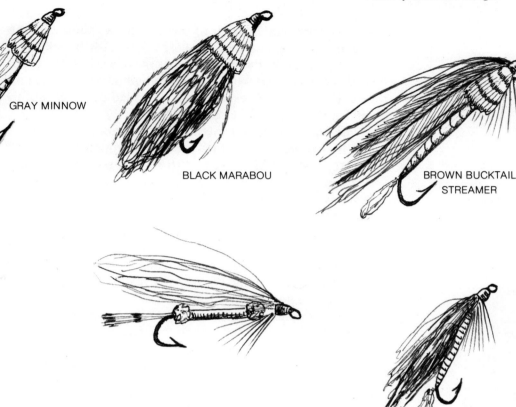

GRAY MINNOW

BLACK MARABOU

BROWN BUCKTAIL
STREAMER

BLACK BUCKTAIL

## *Streamers and Bucktails*

Whenever I think of streamers and bucktails, I remember my friend Jo Bates. He's done a magnificent book on these flies that should be in your angling library. *Streamer Fly Fishing* is a classic.

Streamers and bucktails are imitations of stream and lake minnows upon which the trout feed. They represent an entirely different approach to fly fishing than wet, dry, and nymph fishing. The flies are bigger and heavier, demanding stouter rods and heavier leaders. To be most effective, the flies are fished deep, utilizing the same basic tactics as outlined for the wet fly, but it is necessary that they be sunk deep down and fished erratically, in the imitation of a darting minnow. There is also the dead drift style of presentation that is quite effective, especially in slow water. The trout know that minnows abound all around them. They seldom, if ever, will chase after them unless the minnows are cornered or injured or can be taken at close range by surprise. The little flashers are just

too fast for them. Schools of these minnows abound in the stream pockets, and that is where the trout will seek them out. On the other hand, the lure of the chase is in the brain of every trout, and when he sees something that looks and acts like a minnow, especially a wounded one, he's apt to fall for the ruse and chase after it.

The big point of this method is to have a fly that swims in a lifelike manner in the water. Unfortunately, many of the store-bought flies are tied to sell fishermen. Most are tied too full and fluffy. The correct action is found in a sparsely dressed fly that will have more wiggle and wobble when the right motion reaches it from the rod tip. In many instances, a pattern such as the yellow and red Mickey Fin with the silver body is a killer. This is a bucktail, not a streamer. The Gray Ghost streamer is basically a drab gray color and is made of streamer feathers from a cock's neck. There have been infinite patterns designed as bucktails or streamers, and my friend (and famous angler) Larry Koller designed what he termed the bucktail streamer: a combination of both feathers and deer hair.

As to which is better, the classic feathered streamer, the bucktail, or the combination, this is a matter of choice first and the ability of the angler to make whichever one he chooses do the trick. There are times, obviously, when one seems to work and the other doesn't. Many factors enter here. Color, size, manner of action, and of course, the mood of the trout that are in the vicinity. This might seem very vague to you, but these elements add up to the decisions of fly selection and presentation.

The basic presentation methods are similar to wet-fly and nymph fishing, but a longer, more powerful rod is recommended if the angler wishes to fish longer than average casts. In deep stream work in the early season when it is desired to fish the fly well down on the bottom, the fly and also the leader can be weighted as shown in the wet-fly section. Some anglers even use a sinking fly line to accomplish this. I do not recommend this since the line is difficult to retrieve. It is enough if the leader sinks and the fly line stays afloat. You can use the floating line as an indicator of the strike, though usually the strike to a moving fly is obvious and quick and sometimes quite hard. The roll-pickup cast and quick recast is a favorite technique of mine, especially when fishing over a hot spot. The repetition of the appearance of the fly will many times bring the biggest fish to the rise, and that's the one I'm after!

It has been said by many who swear by the streamer-bucktail school that bigger fish, generally, are taken on these flies, which accounts for their popularity. They are not a cure-all. There have been hours of my time spent in careful fishing with them when I've not had even a flashing tumble or a nip of a strike. At other times, the big boy has come to the fly a split second after it hit the water. Such is the luck with these flies.

The patterns and manner of dressing are the first consideration, and I list some of my favorites in the following table. A few suggestions to fit them are included for presentation.

### STREAMERS AND BUCKTAILS

| Name | Hook | Tail | Body | Wings | Under-hackle | Cheek |
|------|------|------|------|-------|--------------|-------|
| *Streamers* | | | | | | |
| Gray Minnow | 12 long | None | Silver | Gray fur | None | Gray mallard |
| Brown Minnow | 12 long | None | Gold | Brown bucktail | None | Gray mallard |
| Silver Minnow | 12 long | None | Silver | Polar bear and black-and-white mixture | None | Gray mallard |
| Black Marabou | 10 long | None | None | Black marabou | None | Gray mallard |
| Black-and-White Marabou | 10 long | None | None | Black and white marabou | None | None |
| Brown-and-Red Marabou | 10 long | None | None | Brown and red marabou | None | None |
| *Bucktails* | | | | | | |
| Brown Bucktail | 8 long | Red tag | Gold | Brown bucktail | Red | None |
| Black Bucktail | 8 long | Red tag | Silver | Black/brown bucktail | Red | None |

## STREAMERS AND BUCKTAILS (Cont.)

| Name | Hook | Tail | Body | Wings | Under-hackle | Cheek |
|------|------|------|------|-------|--------------|-------|
| *Bucktails (cont.)* | | | | | | |
| Gray Bucktail | 8 long | Red tag | Silver | Gray fur or dyed gray bucktail | Red | None |
| Silver Bucktail | 8 long | Red tag | Silver | Blue-black and white bucktail | Red | None |
| Brown Bucktail-Streamer | 12 long | White tag | Gold | Brown bucktail over brown hackle | Red | Gray mallard |
| Gray Bucktail-Streamer | 12 long | White tag | Silver | Gray bucktail on gray hackle | Red | Gray mallard |
| Mickey Finn Bucktail | 12 long | None | Silver | Red bucktail on top, orange bucktail underneath | Yellow | None |
| Royal Coachman Bucktail | 10 long | Golden pheasant | Peacock and red | White hackle | Brown | None |

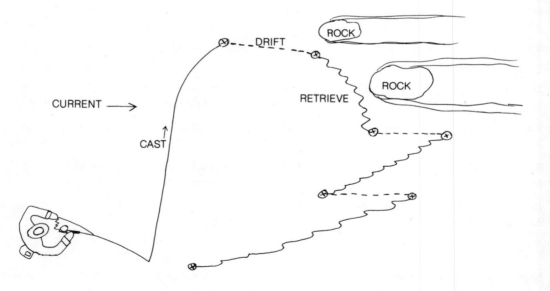

# 5
# Some Shorts on Tackle

Are long leaders necessary? Under most conditions, yes. A long leader, if it is handled properly, will be less likely to put down fish than a shorter leader just as well handled. The long leader, however, is not the end of all problems. It is the beginning of many, and its use demands some drastic changes in line and rod handling. A long leader can extend the cast at least twice the length of itself. A forty-foot cast with a nine-foot leader is forty-nine feet, but a fifty-foot cast with a twelve-foot leader can pull out to an almost mythical seventy feet.

And have you ever tied and used a double-tapered leader?

More on that later.

Arbitrarily, leaders are not made in conventional and standardized sizes any longer than the usual rods. Most of them come in seven-, eight-, and nine-foot lengths. Anglers used to tie their leaders with the loop end to the line, and the rig would not go through the tip-top guides, so the manufacturers limited the sizes and lengths of leaders. That's the only reason they are not longer. But if you tie your own, forget the formats of convention and use as long a leader as you can handle. It will take a good

deal of line taper changing and even the use of a heavier line. Many anglers cut back on the line taper, preferring to butt in a heavier section of leader to replace the line. This is good, and if the taper is of the proper design, a few feet of extremely fine leader can be added. To get the most from this kind of leader its restrictions have to be known and respected.

One has to keep in mind that the flexibility of fly line and leader material vary greatly. The object is to find a point in the line diameter which matches the proper leader material and thickness in order to make an even section for the cast. A heavy line section tied to a light leader section simply will not produce the desired effect, nor will a heavy butt leader tied to an exceptionally fine line end. By properly tying in the leader to the line, the old-fashioned leader loop is eliminated, and, believe it or not, this is a great advantage in the cast, and the rig will also go through the tip-top rod guide when it comes time to bring in the trout.

To produce a long leader requires constant casting of the new designs in order to test them through experimentation. To produce a good twelve-foot leader, for example, is comparatively easy. It cannot be prescribed since there are too many variable factors: the caster's habits, the ac-

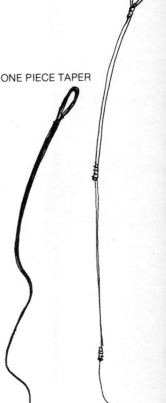

TIED TAPER

ONE PIECE TAPER

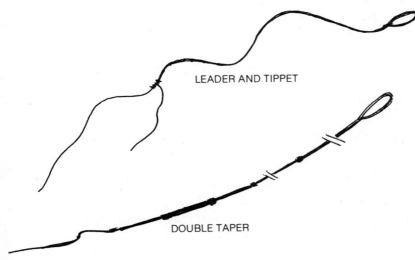

LEADER AND TIPPET

DOUBLE TAPER

tion and length of the rod in *his* hands, and the quality and resilience of the leader material being used. The only way I've ever found the right measurements for a leader was by trial and error. Then, if I wished to duplicate the product, I'd whip out the micrometer and find out just what I had put together. For example: Take a weight-forward, tapered line. Attach an appropriate leader to it. Cast it. If it handles well, go on from there with the experiment. Attach a two-foot length of leader to the butt end of the "boughten" tapered leader. Tie this on the line. Cast it. Does it cast as well as the shorter leader? Yes? Fine. Now, go one step further. Add two feet of thinner leader to the tip end. Cast that. If it is okay, you have now added four feet to the leader without altering the fly line at all. Nine plus four is thirteen feet, and you can quit while you're ahead or go on further.

But before going ahead, jut how versatile is that new thirteen footer? Tie on a size 12 dry and cast it. Okay? Fine. Now tie on a size 18. What happens? Sure, you had to slow down your cast. You'll also have to slow down the cast a good deal if you were to use a size 12 Royal Coachman fan wing.

How is it in a breeze? Can you control it? If not, then chop off two feet of the line and tie in again. Now try it. That's better. Might even try going two more feet of leader at the butt and cut off about two feet of line. That usually works better.

And now, how about distance? Does the new leader cast the fly as far as the original leader did? Does the fly flatten out on the back cast in proper timing and lay out flat and drop down *first* on the water? If so, you are in luck.

You'll notice that you'll have to change your casting timing considerably to accommodate the longer leader. You'll also be throwing a wider bow than you did before, but that is okay.

Now, to really experiment, try a double-tapered leader.

Start where you did before, with a conventional tapered leader (one piece, of course). Cut off about two feet of the butt end and tie on to the line. Now, take off two feet of the end. Now, get a fresh leader and put the micrometer to the end of the leader that's now on the line and work the mike from the thin end to the same measurement as you go toward the butt. Tie this to the first leader and when you reach the end of the leader, select still another and tie it in, butt to butt, so that it will taper down to a thin tipped again. Look at the diagram—it is easier to follow than the words.

The long, double-tapered leader can start at the top of the weight-forward tapered line. From that heavy section, the leader is tapered down to a medium weight and built up again in the forward section of the leader and then down again to the leader tip, as shown. This is a good rig for distance casting over big steelhead waters and particularly for Atlantic salmon on wide expanses where wind is constantly blowing.

You will seldom see a double-tapered leader in use . . . most anglers have never heard of them. I discovered this trick when I was experimenting with spinning gear in the early days. I'd taken one of my old fly rods, cut off the tip by about a foot, and tied on the regulation spinning guides. I used spinning line as the level running line, tied in a section of the bullet-tapered fly line to the heaviest point, and then "went down" with leader to the desired point. That rig cast well with my fly-spinning rod, and the running line on a spinning reel offered no casting and coiling problems. The line would go out, high, and the double-tapered leader would push out straight up in the air, trailing the light tippet. The fly would then trickle down on the water, well after the line of course, but at this distance, who cares?

All of this shows that there is no limit to where you can go in leader design, a relatively unexplored territory in precision dry-fly fishing. We have concentrated, and rightly so, on rods and tapers and lines. But leaders have been left pretty much like the ones granddaddy used. It's time for a change here, for I believe that when enough anglers experiment with longer leaders, their demands on lines will become more specific, and with a change in line design, perhaps there will come some basic changes in rod actions, particularly the last two or three feet of rod.

We've a lot to learn in so-called balanced tackle. Our problem-solving technique has been to start arbitrarily with one end or the other and try to make them match to derive the best from all three elements.

One element which I think has been a drawback in real progress is the demand for distance. It is a great show when an angler can perform for the audience, making those beautiful-looking long casts. Most of the time, in actual fishing, it is all but impossible to control the fly at those distances, and any angler who is a long-line addict will tell you about the fish that have risen to his fly which he was unable to hook, or if he could make the long cast, he couldn't control the fly and help it to drift for a longer time. Had he waded closer to the target and made a

shorter cast, he could have accomplished the job easier and with more dispatch.

I maintain that a longer leader is less visible to the fish, and so with a longer leader and one that I can control, there is less need for that distance, since the line disturbance will be less. Some day, and I bet it won't be a long time either, the line companies will produce a line that will be line in name only. It will be one long leader, all in one piece, and tapered to suit.

## What the Hell Is a Fly Rod?

I'd sure like to know the answer to this question, and I've been fly fishing for some fifty years, have owned and disowned at least twenty-five rods, and am still trying to find out what those experts are talking about.

I can remember once seeing a wild kind of expert demonstrate his casting ability in the casting pool of the New York Sportsmen's Show in the days when it was staged in Grand Central Station. This man was able, by some sleight-of-wrist-and-arm, to make fifty- to sixty-foot casts *without any rod*!

Years later, Ted Trueblood ran a story in *Field & Stream* on his ability to cast very far and well, using a broomstick with, as I remember, the broom still on it!

To my mind, a fly rod should be able to cast a fly at least fifty feet in a wind and be able to turn over a long leader properly so that the fly lands on the water first before the leader and line. With a weight-forward rope line on a long cast, this presents a pretty tough problem.

The rod must have a stiff enough tip to do this job, yet a soft enough tip to avoid too strong a strike that will bust the gossamer leader I use with midges. Yet, it must have enough backbone to lift a long line from the water and be able to roll cast for my quick pickup or line mending that I like to do when I'm fishing across stream.

It must handle a fan-wing Royal Coachman in size 10 and a size 22 midge. If you think I'm going to ape those experts who are constantly recommending different rods for specific purposes, I'm not. I would have to hire a caddy or float a boat full of tackle behind me on the water.

You see a lot of fly fishermen whisk their rods back and forth strenuously in their false casts in order to dry their flies or impress themselves or others watching. They are in love with the performance and have read from Charles Ritz of the advantages of the narrow bow versus the wide bow. His contention, of course, is well grounded.

Since I've switched to the dry fly while using my pet rod designed for streamer and bucktail fishing (a rod I like for

midging, for example) or my dad's fifty-year-old soft and whippy Hardy, of the kind that was fine for Halford, I look at my stiff sticks designed for dry-fly fishing with a sort of laugh. Sure, they work well and so do the others.

My only recommendation for the fly rod is one which will throw a line that is balanced to it to a distance of at least fifty feet. Beyond that distance you are only casting for the audience and your own ego. You can't handle a fly properly beyond that point, and I don't care if the Joe Brooks's school objects. I'll hook twice as many fish at forty feet and twice that number again at thirty feet. I'll leave that sixty footer for the guy on the other bank.

There's a lot of nonsense written about fly rods just like the equally senseless arguments about the relative merits of the 270 over the 30/06 rifles. There isn't a guy alive who can shoot the difference in hunting game. But it sure makes fodder for the after-dinner experts who are talking a comfortable distance from the stream.

And I don't intend to bore you here with a lot of gobbledygook on tapers. I'm too old for such nonsense. Just learn to cast, buddy. You can deliver any fly with a broomstick.

I believe that we tend to concentrate far too much on the design of the rod and not enough on the variable pressures under which the rod will be flexed. These variables include the height of the person holding the rod, how deep he is in the water, how far he expects to cast. A short man deep in the water will not reach as far out with a short rod as he will with a long one. A tall man fishing in shallow water with a long rod will be in a very good equation.

Try to consider the amount of pickup strength and power that will be needed. This is as important to casting as casting is itself. Without the proper pickup, a good cast cannot be made easily. Also, the pace of the casting usually dictates the use of the rod's taper. If you like a zip-zip-zip kind of quick-trigger false cast, this demands a stiffer and/or shorter rod. If you like, as I do, to have a more leisurely paced action, a longer and softer rod is better. This is my choice for long hours of fishing pleasure.

Also, there is the most important element of manipulating the rod's action by the manner in which you apply the pressures in casting. This is a subtle thing, and a sensitivity is needed to master and transfer that impulse to the rod.

Take any rod, and by mentally and thereby physically imparting the action directed to a specific section of the rod, you can create your own style of rod. Try the following exercise.

With about forty feet of line and a ten-foot leader, cast the line easily and smoothly, without exerting any distinct pressure—just merely wave the cast back and forth. Next step is to try and concentrate your wrist action and arm power to activate the very tip of the rod. Try this a few times until you begin to see this work. Now, for contrast, place your concentration just above the handle in the butt section and work the rod from there, allowing the rest of the rod its freedom. You'll note that the rod bends more at the butt and is almost straight from there on out to the tip. Now, place the accent in the middle section of the rod. By practiced manipulation, you have created three distinct rod actions from the one rod. With this sensitivity behind you, you can take a soft whippy rod and turn it into a fast stick and vice versa. Try a fast-action rod, for example, and by concentrating on the very tip section, it becomes much slower. Put your action attention in the butt and it becomes abnormally fast. With all this now in your consciousness, you can take any rod and throw anything from bucktails to tiny dry flies, casting well all the way.

So I repeat that we should try to really get to know all of the subtleties of the rods we look at and try out. Trying to find a rod that fits all our needs is an impossibility, while one rod properly known and used along the lines suggested here will fulfill almost all needs of the most particular angler. With new rod materials coming on the scene, we might then be more able to develop tapers that make much better sense.

If you find in your hands a rod with a stiff butt and middle section and a limber tip portion, you can, by the above manipulation, pressure the lower part of the rod, leaving the tip to follow through. If the rod is soft all over, you can either stiffen it up in the butt section or the tip by careful pressuring on the cast. In effect, then, to a large degree *you* control the power sections of your rod and will be able then to bring out the best in the rod's action at will for all kinds of conditions, such as a line that is too heavy, leaders that are long and light or short and thick, flies that whizz through the air with little resistance, or the big fan wings that tend to slow down your cast.

With all this mastered, you can then be more persnickety about the *basic* action you want and can manipulate. You'll find these techniques in few other fishing books in your library.

# 6
# Wading a Trout Stream

You are fishing with me as we approach the lower end of a
wide pool that is graced by a potent bit of water known as
a shelving riffle. Over to the left, the water is thin and
shallow—and fast. But out in the middle is the drop-off
which turns in a slim S-shape down the center. Over on the
right is a grassy bank with overhangs and undercut banks.

The best water is, of course, the drop-off where the flat
current bogs down into a deep run. If we watch that water
for a few minutes, we'll see trout flashing on the bottom,
probably feeding on caddis larvae. Later, perhaps, those
trout that reside there will be nosing right to the lip of the
drop-off, all along the line to the top of the pool. They'll
be there because flies are hatching well upstream and drifting down right into their mouths. Or, perhaps, there will
be a hatch right then and there, and they'll be in the right
place for it.

As we watch from our station at the bottom of the pool,
an angler enters from the left. He comes out from the
brush, sloshes across the shallow water about midway
down the stretch. He stops just at the lip of the drop-off
and begins to cast downstream and across with what looks
like a brace of wet flies. After a few minutes of this, he

switches to dry flies and now wades right into the deep part of the run and begins to cast his dry flies toward the head of the pool. He gets strikes from two small trout and, apparently deciding to go elsewhere, he proceeds to turn around and stop casts his dry flies downstream into the water below which he has just waded through. Finally, after a few more casts, he reaches us as we are still waiting for the end of the show before we fish that pool properly.

"This pool used to produce some mighty fine trout, but I guess those days are gone," he says during our brief conversation.

We wait until the pool has had a few minutes to settle. Soon the trout again begin to flash near the bottom, and we proceed, not up the center but well off to the left, in that shallow, fast waste water. We cast wet flies and nymphs upstream and across, landing our lines just to the left of the drop-off so that the flies dribble down into the deep. And we get action!

We have only waded up about a quarter of the length of the pool when a couple of trout rise to what appears to be hatching insects above them. We switch to dry flies, casting in the same manner: up and slightly across the fast current to drop the drys right on the drop-off lip.

Zap! We're on!

Gradually we work our way up the left side of the pool to cast right into the head of the pool. From this position, the dry flies can enjoy a long float, all the way from the tip of the pool to as far downstream as practicable.

As we glance below, another angler is about to work his way up. We proceed to the next pool. Our new friend below has the pool now. It is undisturbed and the fish are feeding.

Now, let's take a look at another typical situation.

The center rock. Our pool is a long one with a great big rock right in the center of it. This is one of the most over-worked areas of any trout stream, and most of the time it is approached in the wrong way—not arbitrarily, but simply because many of us are sometimes in much too much of a hurry to get into the water. If we could just stand on the sidelines a few seconds and plan an approach, chances are we wouldn't even have to set foot in the water.

For example: Suppose that center rock is a nice forty-five–foot cast from the dry gravel on our side of the pool. Would we wade right in? I hope not! First, we'd make a few casts right to the edge of our beach, just in case cruising trout might be there nosing out insects. The current between there and the rock is quite fast and deep. Lots of area to cast to above and below the rock before ever at-

tacking the rock itself. We could spend an hour using everything from dry flies cast into the head of the run to drift down near or right by the rock itself. We could also throw a succulent bucktail up and across and let it sink deep to ride by the rock. As another alternative, we could walk up the beach, well away from the water so as not to put the fish down and cast down and across and then retrieve our flies back to us. Or we could also walk downstream below the rock and quarter our casts up and across, working as close to the rock as we could get.

While we are figuring all this out, an angler who has been walking upstream on the other bank spots the rock as he's just about opposite it. He wades in half way to the rock and begins to cast. We see trout spurt out in all directions. The pool has had it.

Now, these are only two examples of how and how not to approach the water. The idea is to use our sense of observation and to plan our strategy accordingly and spare the pool and be in a position to cast our flies properly to fish that are not driven away from their station or put off feed.

I'm not against wading. No way. But, just because we own a pair of waders is no guarantee that we'll catch our limit of fish.

Ownership of a pair of waders is an open invitation to wade right in (if you'll excuse the expression) where angels and anglers should fear to tread.

Good, safe wading can make the difference between hits and no hits. Take, for example, a stretch of water with big boulders and fast, deep runs and water that churns so much that you cannot see the bottom clearly. The bottom of the river is quite uneven, like a crosscut saw. It is consistently dangerous in that any gravel stretches among the rocks are always unsteady due to the pressures of the water. Some of the rocks can be dislodged if you walk on their tops, or in wading, knock them off balance. Add to this the pressure of the water forcing anything in its path into submission and you have the makings of a broken ankle or at least a cold wetting.

So, before thinking of fishing this stretch, let's take into consideration just what we are getting in for when we venture forth. And venture we must, for in order to fish it properly we must place ourselves in a position for certain drifts and angles of proper presentation.

To wade this or any water, be it in a trout stream or in a lake or even the rocky shoreline of the ocean or inlet, the selection of proper wading gear is fully as important as the choice of rod and line. A few years ago, comfortable and adequate wading equipment at a reasonable price was practically unheard of, but now manufacturers have developed waders that are not only durable and waterproof but actually featherweight. Some companies manufacture waders in three weights: heavy, medium, and light. The heavyweight type offers years and years of wear but are more bulky and hot. The medium weights are what the name implies and are recommended for the sometimes fisherman who doesn't tend to go hard on his togs. The lightweight variety are for the occasional angler who will be careful where he wades.

The basic material has always been rubber, either all rubber or rubberized fabric. The most modern development is the use of the newer plastics. In the early days, these waders used to split unmercifully at the seams but now, for the most part, if the waders are not stretched unduly, they will hold up very well.

Waders come in three lengths: hip-boot height, just like

hip boots, waist-highs, and armpit length, for the really deep wading.

Correct fit is the major consideration in the selection of your wading gear. If your build is such that the regulation waders will not fit properly, don't buy any waders unless you are willing to pay the price of a factory-fitting job. Waders that are too tight in the crotch will split, particularly when you are stretching to the safety of an overhanging limb or crossing a windfall along the trail. Waders that are too deep or too loose in the crotch are even worse, because they tend to restrict leg movement.

There are two styles of foot: boot foot and stocking foot. The boot foot is more common, since it takes less time to get in and out of them. Also, various kinds of sandle bottoms can be purchased to fit the types of water to be waded. The stocking-foot waders demand a pair of wool socks over the outside and a large pair of wading brogues, heavy shoes with the desired clamp-ons for added grip.

As to wading technique, a few general rules will help to make the chore easier, safer, and more pleasurable. Do not walk in the water as you do on land. Do not "step" as you do on land. Slide your feet from rock to rock or through the gravel, feeling the bottom with your feet, and always keep your balance on the back foot until you are certain that the lead foot is solidly in place. Most of the time currents fuzz up the water and reflections prevent you from seeing the bottom ahead of you with any clarity. It is very easy to step into a hole if your balance is not on the back foot. Also, take small steps and, when wading upstream, quarter against the current on an angle. It is easier than merely walking straight up against it. In downstream wading, take the same type of angle so that the push of the water is gliding by you instead of trying to push you downstream faster than you wish to go.

After a few spills and a few almost-spills, you'll appreciate the merits of taking it easy and, again, learning to plan your moves. You'll then fully appreciate the great advantages there are to proper wading. Use the art with respect.

I can recall many times when wading was an advantage and also when it was unnecessary.

During the war when gasoline was rationed, I used to

measure it with a tea cup. I'd drive to the stream and fish as long a stretch during the weekend as my strength allowed. It was tiring to walk great distances with waders. So after a long hike down the railroad tracks, I'd be pretty tired, and the prospect of battling currents wasn't of the strongest appeal. So I'd clamber over the boulders along the stream and make my casts from shore. Given the extra height, I'd be able to cast well out into the pools and long deep runs. Also, I could see the trout when they were flashing under water, feeding on the bottom, usually on caddis cases. When they'd become active, I'd see this show from a high vantage point and pick my techniques accordingly. It was surprising how much fun it was to fish without even entering the water as I had been used to doing. I learned the fascinating art of the roll cast and perfected it to the limit, also learning the roll-pickup cast and the roll-cast strike, but that is another story. But it happened because I was too tired to broach those deep river runs.

But I quickly forgot the lesson on the days when I was refreshed and would arbitrarily and without thinking walk right to the stream and enter it, forgetting that I could fish from the shore *first* before entering the water. I had the wading habit, like so many others, and took wading as a matter of course. I'd wade out into the stream even before rigging up a special leader and selected flies for the occasion. It was a bad habit and one which drained me of much energy needlessly.

Then one day I hooked my ankle into a piece of submerged barbed wire and immediately felt the cold wet stream on my foot. I waded ashore immediately and took off the waders. Without a patching kit I was out of business or so I thought. It was too long a hike back to the inn where I was staying; so I had only one alternative to returning to the local garage for a patch and that was to stay ashore and learn to fish from there.

Ahead of me was a long stretch of open water with shallows and deeper runs. It was all in the open, affording plenty of room for long back casts. So I picked my way, walking from rock to rock as close to the stream edges as possible, false casting and alternately dropping the flies into the likely runs. It was surprising how much water I could cover from the shore, and I learned to fish stretches of stream that I'd have skipped over if I'd been wading in the center of the river. And I took trout.

What had started out as being a sad restriction was the opening of an entirely new phase of fishing for me. It was amazing how much good water I'd been missing from my usual position in midstream.

Another thing I noticed was that if I were to wade out in the center of the stream, I'd be casting to the pockets along the shore, for anyone who has ever studied insects knows that many of them hatch and live on the stream banks and edges and the trout go there for them when they are hungry.

Now I could cover those stream edges and undercut banks with ease, and sometimes I could hold on to an old tree and dapple my fly under its overhanging branches right into the mouth of a big trout—a feat that I had difficulty managing from a hip-deep position well out from the tree. And I took trout.

It reminded me of the days before I could afford a pair of waders or for that matter had ever heard of them. I fished for years in sneakers and long pants, wading in only when necessary.

Then the day came when I could afford a pair of boots, and my, what a change in my life. Now I could wade out quite a bit from the stream edge and make casts into those deep runs in the center of the stream. I felt as if I'd been set free in a new land. Added to this was tackle that could perform casts in an unbelievable way. I had the entire stream licked, but as I recall, I didn't catch any more fish than before, but I was now wading the stream, just like those experts pictured in the sporting magazines.

But wading in boots taught me a lesson most anglers never learn since they start out with waders. You have to wade carefully and try and keep from rolling stones and slipping and sliding all over the bottom, since your margin in shorter boots is not as generous as in armpit waders. You learn care, and you also learn to plan your wading path with caution. More often than not, careless planning can lead you onto a reef or bar, especially if it is pointed downstream. Out there you cannot cross through the deeper water in order to reach the shore; so you have to wade upstream against a strong current and that can be fatiguing to say the least. For those who don't think or plan ahead, I recommend waders.

Waders are not only a material luxury but an emotional one. Not that I'm against owning waders for I have three pairs of them, but when wading becomes more important than fishing strategy, then it is better to restrict one's self.

Aging has its effect in helping to realize the merits of proper wading and the planning of a wading path up a given stretch of water. When you get to the age when you are spelling *natures* backwards, then you really begin to count your steps and conserve your energies. For me, gone are the days when I could be seen in the wildest parts of the river, wading into and through very dangerous water. Even some of my astute angling partners considered me a maniac in waders. It seems that part of my enjoyment of fishing was to lick the power of the stream. Sure I caught fish where and when they didn't, but that's not the point here.

In short, a lot of wading is really not necessary, and if the angler will take the time to look over the water about to be fished and plan his moves with a bit of caution and a bit of laziness, he'll see that he'll likely have more fishing action due to the fact that wading *does* put fish down. Of this there is no question. Trout, particularly trout that are waded over by many anglers during a given day, become scared—not just wary—plumb scared. It is amazing how many trout disappear from a pool or go off feed when waders put down their first steps in to the pool. If you have ever watched a pool from a bridge and seen the results of fishermen wading up the middle, you'd know what I mean. Even if they wade quietly and slowly, the fish know all about it and take cover. No matter how many scientifically tied flies and super tackle are employed in perfectionist casts, it is of no account if the trout have finned their way to the water of elsewhere.

On a stream where one fisherman is following another, unless they wade *very* quietly and slowly, the fishing is bound to be nil if there are no trout there to entice.

On the other hand, a fisherman who can wade step by step, slowly, hardly ever pounding the bottom but slithering his feet along stealthily, will more often than not see trout feeding almost under his rod tip. Many times, after standing in one spot for several minutes, I've glanced behind me to see trout that have taken up positions in my wake. I've had trout grab mayflies within inches of my waders, and one time I had a trout rise to a fly beside my landing net and pounce right into it!

Now, all this good wading strategy, particularly that of *not wading,* adds to our fishing fun and knowledge fund. It also puts less strain on the bottom with obvious conservation of the stream insects.

Own good waders and use them, but wisely and sparingly. You'll see that your fishing prowess will improve, and you'll get to know the stream better if you wade less and fish more. And, the less you wade, the better the trout stream will be for it.

# 7
# Back to Fundamentals

Only an old codger like me can appreciate the wondrous modern-day tackle available to everyone who wants to learn to fish and at a price he can easily afford. If you look at tackle development and outdoor gear available for trips afield over the past twenty-five years, you are looking at the marvel of the ages. Tackle and gear design has evolved toward perfection more than it did in the preceding two-hundred years, and it's still getting better.

Take fly rods, for example. For just a few dollars you can buy a rod that will cast sixty feet with ease. You hardly have to care for it like we had to baby the rods of long ago. And good action? Every conceivable taper has been designed to please all kinds of tastes and supply the right action for almost every conceivable need.

And lines . . . no need to continually dress them to float. They will float forever. And we have lines that sink at the tip and sink all over. Rods are tapered to fulfill the most exacting needs for the effortless delivery at long distances. Leaders, likewise.

And flies? There have never been so many scientifically designed flies—far cries from the old school—for these are not made just to look pretty. Some of the newer ones look more like insects than the insects do.

It would seem then that everyone who buys an outfit and reads what the experts advise would likewise become an expert. We'd be producing McClanes, Hidys, Schwieberts, Foxes, and Swishers by the dozens. The trout would be in serious trouble.

How come we don't?

Perhaps it is because the focus on tackle and tackle performance plus the ease of getting to and from good fishing places has led us to believe that fish will result simply because we have acquired the tackle and the transport. Maybe all this good gear has spawned a generation of fly fishermen who do not recognize the need to learn the fundamentals. Casting performance is one thing. Fish count is something else.

How come those of us who caught trout fifty years ago did so without all this magnificent tackle and few books to read on the subject? Perhaps it was because we had to be fundamentalists. We operated at a slower pace and put our attention on observation and reading the water, rather than depending on our gear to catch the trout.

Going fishing today is a big production of gear assembly and sorting out equipment and flies. But I can remember when "goin' fishin' " was a pleasure. That was before I became technical about it all and wealthy enough to afford all the scientific makings of an outdoor excursion. I spent many years trying to discover all the secrets that lay beneath the currents and much midnight oil developing lures and flies that I was certain would take fish. And tackle? I could quote you the measurements of every foot of rod taper, every line dimension, and length of taper. My leaders were all measured with the same precision. I knew all the hatches on my favorite trout streams. I caught trout when others couldn't or didn't, and I had a ball!

I wrote books (too many, some people think) about all this and was considered to be an expert when asked to be the after-dinner speaker at fishing clubs. And speaking as a man of near retirement age, I wouldn't have missed a minute of it!

But, they say, when you get to the leisure world, retired class, you become simpleminded. Perhaps this is so, but the condition bears a strange resemblance to the days before and during puberty—days spent with a simple "pole" and line, dime-store hook, and worms or hoppers for bait—or the times when soaking leaders the night before a trip was a part of the ritual—or when I'd walk out on the cabin porch before going to bed to try to ascertain what the weather would be like on the morrow.

Wet-fly fishing was a pleasure then. No one had complicated it with nymph fishing! All one had to do to attach flies to the leader was to slip the loop in and over the leader loop, and presto! you were in business. If you wanted to change flies, no problem; merely disengage the loop and replace with another pre-snelled fly. They worked. They caught fish and big ones too. But don't be seen with one of them on today's modern stream!

The rods didn't cast as far those days, or if they did, it was only after great effort. As a result, the fishing was more relaxed. I'd merely wade a bit closer to the area to be worked and drop the fly where it was supposed to go. I'd never heard of the narrow bow or the wide bow or the double haul, and it was several years before I bought a double-tapered line. About a dozen flies were all that I carried on the stream . . . in an envelope. I didn't own a fly book or fly boxes. In order not to crush my dry flies, I stuck them in my hat band.

Lake fishing? I'd row an old scow of a boat that was equipped with two lard pails for bailing and a flat rock for an anchor. I used to wade in streams and lakes, barefoot, before the age of discarded pop bottles, zip-lock tops, and a careless generation. I'd drink from the stream or lake, too, without knowing the word *pollution*.

And nightcrawlers. (Taken along in case the flies didn't deliver.) Why, half the sport of fishing was in spending an hour at the local golf course well after dark with a flashlight and a big bottle. Today all I have to do is produce money at the local tackle store. Gathering minnows . . . another great part of fishing, but today the pleasure is robbed by rows of pickled ones in jars or a live tank at the local baitery.

And fishing books. A far cry from those of today. I remember Henry Van Dyke's *Fisherman's Luck* and Izaak Walton's *Compleat Angler,* nothing technical, just pure uncomplicated enjoyment, loaded with philosophy, serenity, and lots of fish!

And reaching the fish. Simple. All I had to do was to

walk down to the river. A more distant one required an hour's peddling on the bicycle. If I wanted to go still further, I routed on several buses or hitched a ride. Camping equipment? Shucks, I carried all I needed under one arm, and I ate all the fish, cooked at stream or lakeside, and nobody reported seeing smoke. There were no No Trespassing signs. As long as you closed the gates, you were O.K.

Then I grew up, had a sample of stiff competition in the door-to-door selling business, a bit of war, and the dress of an executive. My fishing followed suit and became sophisticated. The old simple tackle was long gone. The early books forgotten. I went wild, experimenting with tackle, and read all the biology books and how-to books and sporting magazines, starved for information. When I did take to the water, I needed a station wagon to carry all the size 22 hooks. Fishing was a complicated procedure. I'd spend several minutes with a magnifying glass, identifying a species of mayfly while the trout were gorging themselves in front of me. It would take me months of the off-season to assemble gear and tackle for the coming season. Two hours on the night before opening day, I'd work like a beaver getting all set. By the time I waded into the stream I could have been mistaken for a tackle store.

Then decisions, decisions. What fly? What leader? Which rod? Which reel? Long casts, short casts, wade here, cast there; water temperature, barometer reading, time of year, type of hatch. . . .

Whew! When I think of it now! But I was to have my comeuppance.

Not too long ago I had the roof fall in at the hands of a Maine guide and some pesky squaretail trout. I'd been fishing for almost three days on some of the best upper Allagash River waters: ponds, lake-connecting streams, and the main river itself. Despite some twenty years of solving the problems of capturing sophisticated trout from Catskill and Pennsylvania streams, those gaudy squaretails were giving me the brush-off. My tackle was the tops any man could afford, all balanced to perfection, including long leaders and, if I do say so myself, flies that I'd tied with saintly perfection. The conditions were perfect. Lots of squaretails, as proven by some catches I'd seen made by the locals. Weather? Fine and just the right

temperature. Some fly hatches with whoppers rising to them. But something was wrong, despite my movielike performance. Even my guide was impressed with my gear, my casting prowess, my apparent knowledge of the stream, the hot spots, and the Latin names of the insects I'd catch in between sixty-foot double hauls. But the trout would have none of it.

Then the guide suggested trying his methods and I agreed. We drifted ashore and while still seated in the canoe, the guide unwrapped a heavy looped leader and proceeded to tie it in place of mine. On it were three snelled flies. One roll cast and the rig drifted out and down from the canoe, right into the current. The flies swayed back and forth, lazily.

The next project was to go ashore and light a fire and cook some coffee and then settle down to the facts of living where we were for the night. I helped unload the canoe, forgetting for the moment that the flies were in the water and that my priceless rod was propped up against the center thwart.

As I was about to lug two duffles ashore from the bow of the canoe, I heard the reel grind like a mad rattlesnake. I turned in time to see the rod bending dangerously, the line being pulled out from the reel in staggering pulses. I almost upset the canoe in dropping my duffles and making an awkward swipe for the rod. Once in my hand I felt the first trout action of the trip. Seems a good-sized trout was giving that tackle a real workout, now well downstream. As I gathered in some of the slack and began to pressure the fish there were *two* splashes at the same time. There were *two* fish on that line! Big ones! Finally when I had them about licked, the guide came by wearing a smile on his face that had a message for me.

The same performance went on three more times before the coffee water was hot.

On another occasion I was the guest of Ed Sens whose family had inherited a large land grant, including some choice river on the Catskill's Neversink, just above the famed water belonging to Edward R. Hewitt. Ed was working with me at the time on my first book about fly fishing and wanted me to share some of his experience with big brown trout on his water. I'd been tying flies for several years and had, on the tip of my tongue, the Latin

names of all the insects of those waters. There was little I hadn't learned about scientifically balanced tackle, long leaders, and sophisticated line handling, and the art of fly presentation. When the book came out, I'd be an expert. There was no doubt about it.

Now, Ed's father was also a fisherman. All through dinner he listened to our technical discourses about the life cycles of the mayfly and the merits of certain feather dyes, line tapers, and the problems with fishing long leaders.

He decided to join us for the evening hatch on the river. When I asked him about fishing and how he did it, he didn't offer much except to say that he had a rod out in the barn with some flies on it that he'd tied on the leader about three years ago. They seemed to work for him; so he had never bothered to change them. I asked Ed if he had tied them for his dad, and he said that his father had bought them at the local general store downriver and was quite satisfied with their results.

That evening on the river, those three flies outfished the best Ed and I could manage. The old man stood on a rock in plain sight at the head of the pool while we waded up and down the pool, armpit deep, double hauling to keep our lines from slapping the water.

I can also remember a terrifying experience of falling in and almost drowning in a pool of one of my favorite trout streams. I lost all my fly boxes except the one dry fly that was still attached to the rig I was using before the fall. It was too far to walk back to the hotel, and besides, the only flies for sale in town I considered unfit for panfish.

So I was reduced to fishing the balance of the day with the one fly. And you know what? I caught three brown trout that would be a credit to any expert. I'd been forced into a corner and made to produce from the simple point of utilizing all the stream knowledge I'd picked up over the years and fished that one fly for dear life.

It proved to me that we put our money on too many fly-pattern possibilities. There were too many thirty years ago, and in the last ten years, we authors have further complicated the choice and loaded the market with our own peculiar creations. If it were possible for an angler to go astream with all the possibilities that have been presented as the last word in killing patterns, he'd have to float a suitcase filled with only one copy of each pattern. I wonder if it would be possible to be able to select just one for the leader and if so, what would be the justification for that choice. There are probably more patterns than there are insects from which they have derived their shape and color. Yet, flytiers and anglers continue to invent them and use them and even, at times, catch fish with them. Why?

It is a most dangerous thought, but what if all of this free inventiveness is all nonsense? That would be most devastating to the ego and disastrous to creativity. Heaven forbid that we should learn how to fish instead and then have to rely on only three or four flies that have taken trout consistently under all conditions for the past fifty or hundred years.

So, I wonder sometimes if inventing fly types, styles, and special dressings is not for another purpose—that of trying to carve a niche for ourselves in the lore of angling through the presenting and popularization of something different and supposedly better than that which has come down the pike before us, or is it that we can and likely will fish the new flies designed either by ourselves or some well-publicized expert with more confidence, or is it just that trout fishermen who tie flies are blessed with an overabundance of creativity backed by an insatiable desire to find the pattern that will be the all-time killer.

And as for those "sophisticated trout" . . . I buy the theory that man is slowly evolving and changing, but I can't quite go along with the idea that in a period of a hundred years the trout strains are becoming intellectual and producing wiser fry. You read a lot of drivel about sophisticated trout, trout that are highly selective and leader shy in comparison to their more wildly bred brothers in the backcountry streams. I submit that this sort of thinking clouds the real issues of trouting, even if it does offer a sedative after heading homeward after a day of light hits. It may seem that those fish way back in the wilds will bite anything thrown at them. Such fishing success is common experience. But who knows how many trout were there and what percentage of them were hungry at the time? We must remember that in our open water streams there are comparatively less trout per acre of water. The sparsely populated stream offers more food per fish; so he's not quite so prone to bite at just anything that comes along. On top of that, with wading constantly setting him off balance, he's hiding more often than resting or feeding, and it takes a pool quite a few minutes to return to normal once a man has fished through it.

Take any trout, hatchery or wild bred, and he'll do just what comes naturally. He'll feed on what's available when he's hungry and not feed when he wants to rest or digest his recent meal. The excuse that hatchery fish do not feed like natural-bred fish is not always true. *Both* of them will take a floating fly at times, particularly the hatchery fish, even though he's never read a fly-tying book. I've proven this in a hatchery pond.

No, I cannot buy the theory that trout are smart and we have to outwit them. We have to get back to fundamentals.

This does not mean that we should abandon all kinds of fly-pattern design and development or decry the use of new and supposedly unorthodox fly types in order to present to the trout a morsel that looks to him like the real thing. Neither should we cling to traditions. I know one flytier who would never be caught dead clipping hackles to shape a fly, for example. No way!

If the Swisher-Richards, no-hackle fly does the trick, we haven't outwitted the trout. We have, perhaps, found a new way to present to the trout the likes of a living insect upon which it likes to feed. But that the no-hackle fly is the end of the road (or even the beginning or something special) is a moot point. If it were truly the answer, completely, then where and into what ashcan do we place the Hewitt Bi-visible, no-wing, all-hackle fly or the venerated Gordon Quill or the Royal Coachman?

Certainly I'd never go astream without the old standbys such as the gray hackle, brown hackle, black hackle, and grizzly hackle, wings or no wings, who cares!

It is also strange and interesting that we seem to go round and round in our inventiveness. The no-hackle, SR type fly was invented and used quite a few years ago in France. As a matter of fact, I used them myself in the 1940s when I became too lazy to bother putting on the hackle. I've also used the all-hackle, no-wing flies because I was in too much of a hurry to bother with cocking the wings properly. Recently I developed a dry fly with nothing but a fluffy, furry body, only to find that some angler had written a book about fur flies. I'm sorely tempted to figure a way to float a bare hook if I can find a chemical dressing that will do the trick!

Seriously, though, when we look at the fine old English patterns and the standardized collection of about twenty American dry flies, it would seem to be enough for us.

And all the fuzzy business about specialized tapers of rods and manufacturing techniques and glass versus bamboo nonsense.

Have you ever been forced to fish with strange, borrowed tackle? A friend of mine, bless his heart, is a most generous man but a duffer of a fly fisherman. I was visiting him during a few days off between business prob-

lems, and he offered to lend me his spare tackle so we could go fishing together. The plan was to go down to the river in the late afternoon and try for some trout for supper.

Now, if you've spent years and many dollars in the selecting of perfect tackle, a duffer outfit is not exactly your choice. The rod was wavey and soft. The line didn't match, and the leaders were heavy enough to land a muskie. But we went fishing that day with store-bought flies. He'd read one of my books and expected me to catch a trout on every cast.

And you know what? I didn't take a fish on *every* cast, but I came close to it. To this day I can't remember a time when the dry fly proved so generous. Maybe it was the action of the rod that did it. Anyway, under ordinary conditions I wouldn't have given that fly rod to my worst enemy.

Now, these brief encounters with the luck of the century are not recounted here to put down the expert or to shatter

any illusions. Far be it from me to run down the extreme and heroic efforts of such angling celebrities as Ernie Schwiebert, Pete Hidy, Lee Wulff, Leisenring, McClane, and Zern and their astute knowledge of the entire spectrum of angling know-how. Just to watch them perform is an experience. Likewise the Charlie Foxes, Art Flicks, Ray Bergmans, Joe Brookses, and technicians like Jack Knight. They have all given us a background, an education, a tradition of fine art in trout fishing and an "image." Yet, I've fished with most of them and countless others in the writing game who have been widely acclaimed and published, and I've seen 'em skunked, too! This they won't deny. Some have even succumbed to discarding their size 22 midges in favor of size 6 Royal Coachmen when their scientific know-how was shattered.

Why did they abandon the theory? They returned to fundamentals. Give the trout something that will excite him when he's finicky.

What are some of the basic fundamentals needed for a fair share of strikes and creeled trout? There are but a few.

I maintain that all the entomological knowledge, a degree in marine biology, and a big bank account which allows the buying of much and expensive gear will not replace the simple techniques learned in a season or two by a country boy with the traditional alder pole. It is just that in our modern life-style the simple seems to be the thing shunned in favor of becoming embroiled into the complicated. I always thought we went fishing to get away from complications for the purposes of recreation.

Now, don't start throwing away all those expensive rods and lines or discarding all the fly-tying gear and the racks of books. Just try and remember the sage advice from the sales manager addressing the novice salesmen: "Keep it simple, son."

For example, ninety percent of the time it is unnecessary to make long casts. A lot of trout were caught before the advent of weight-forward lines and the double haul. A simple forty-foot cast is all that is needed most of the time, *if* you have learned *where* to cast that fly and know how to control it. Armpit waders are necessary, but it is not essential to remain submerged all the time. Probably more fish are caught by shallow wading or no wading at all. Most fishermen wade where they should fish and fish where they should wade. As to the choice of fly, don't be taken in by all the fads. The old standbys, just a half dozen of them, have taken tons of trout. Don't panic if you can't match the hatch—a Royal Coachman will sometimes be better.

Don't be taken in by traditions. Fish the dry fly *downstream* once in a while, and don't worry about the classical drag. Skitter the fly in the run, just as you would a wet fly. It just might work even if some expert has not written it so.

Learn to study the water and realize that the secret is out there, not necessarily in the fly box.

Wade quietly with the purpose of placing yourself in the correct casting position without effort.

Trout fishing is more than good tackle ownership and heady knowledge. It is the ability to be relaxed, aware of the stream and its activities, and to relate to what's going on.

Keep the tackle in good shape and don't own too much to the point of confusion, but own tackle that is adaptable to the stream conditions as golf clubs are slated for their specific shots.

And, just for kicks, "keep it simple, son," and you'll enjoy your time astream in a different and broader way. When nobody's looking, we experts do just this, and we better enjoy the simple pleasures of angling.

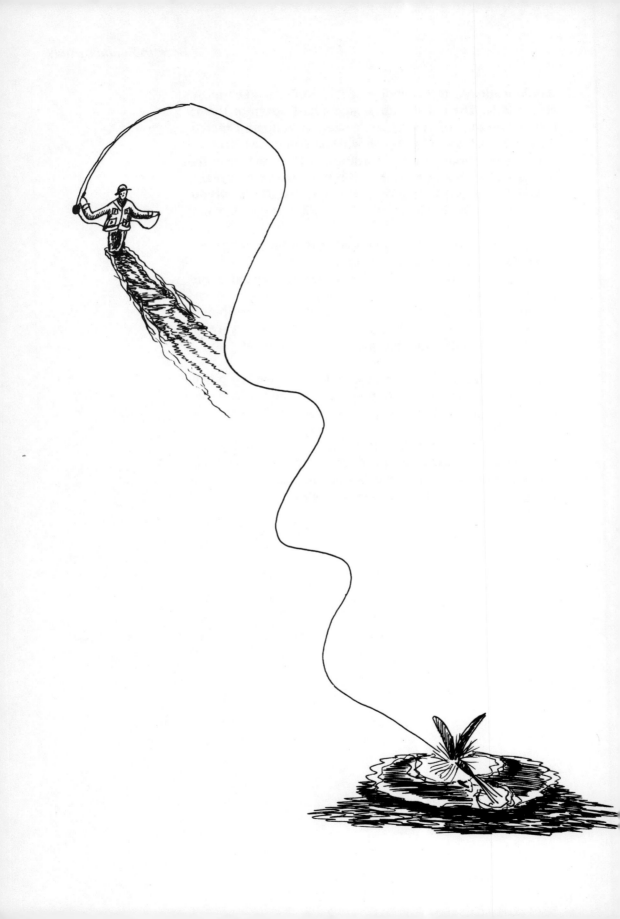

# 8
# On Casting

If you were to put all the written and diagrammed fly-casting instructions that have been printed end to end, they'd probably reach from New York to Peking; so we are not going to put you through the same old course here. Rather, we have a few subtleties to offer that may be new to more recently arrived fly casters and perhaps even a few old-timers who still have a bit to learn.

I've witnessed the casting prowess of a few real experts. I was a youngster the first time I saw George LaBranche cast on the Beaverkill. Ed Hewitt was another from whom I learned. He made long casts to impress the students but short ones when he was after a big trout. In later years it was Eugene V. Connett casting on the famous Pennsylvania Brodheads who impressed me no end, as did John Alden Knight. After you have seen men like these perform, you go to the stream secretly and work for hours to try and perfect the same kind of ease, grace, and precision that marks them as the real pros.

Two elements are required. First, the right combination of rod, reel, line, and leader for the conditions of the moment. If the balance is not perfect for *your particular strength and power and personality,* you won't cast like they do. The second part is practice—to the tenth power. No way is it possible to cast a fly like an expert in ten easy sessions as is promised by many positive-thinking authors who fail to realize that what they write about took them many impatient hours and even years to perfect. It is easy to write the how-to stuff but quite another matter for the reader when he goes forth, even if well equipped, quite aware, and well coordinated.

I think one of the most devastating hangups in the fly-rod brotherhood is an insane desire to make long casts, *too* long casts. Sure, it is necessary once in a while to reach way out there to a spot not reachable in any other way, but by and large, the smart dry-fly fisherman knows that beyond fifty feet he has little or no control over his cast once it lies out on the water. Sure, he'll get many rises to his floater, merely because it is there, but unless the trout hooks himself, the creel will remain empty. The best and most productive dry-fly fishing, at least for the man who wades quietly and approaches his stream problem with any kind of awareness, is accomplished from forty or forty-five feet. This is a good compromise when using a six- to eight-foot rod and a ten-foot leader. If the angler can handle a fifteen-foot leader well, then that extra five feet should be sufficient for almost any circumstance.

When I have taught casting, I've tried to impress beginners and a few old-timers that if they can master, to within inches, their dry fly and place it properly in the current either directly upstream with little or no slack or across the stream with adequate extra bend in the line for a short drift or quartering downstream with sufficient slack but not an over supply, they will have the game under control. It is of little use to cast a line directly upstream with snakelike slack drifting immediately back on the water. What if a fish hits? You have to haul back hard to absorb the slack and set the hook. By that time, the trout has hit the fly, rejected it, and is halfway across the pool before you have tightened the line. It is better then to have quick control over your line. Sure, cast as far out as you can while still controlling the line in the drift. This can vary, since the speed of the water coming down the pool is going to have a definite effect on your line and the amount you can afford to cast. If, for example, the stream flow is fast, a direct upstream cast of long length is going to be largely a waste of time. Better to make a shorter cast where you can control the line. If you wish to reach out farther, *wade up* and then make your shorter cast.

This advice usually falls on deaf ears and the angler has to discover this himself. It is like the first-day boater who runs the craft at full speed to see how fast it will go, or the kid with a hot rod who enjoys burning rubber when leaving the filling station. He'll find that most of his town and city driving will be under the forty-mile-an-hour mark.

The only way to increase the distance and still be able to keep the line well in control is to go armed with a much longer and thus heavier rod. This will, if balanced with the right line and leader, add perhaps five feet to your practical range of casting. But it will not eliminate the problem of all that line on the water that, if left slack, will cause the trout's strike to be missed.

But there are very few of us who can handle a big rod hour after hour and maintain direction and accuracy under the fatigue that a big rod causes.

Since many dry-fly anglers prefer the lightest rods possible, this long-distance thing is more for the grandstand than for serious angling, with the exception, of course, being the once-in-a-while cast to a spot impossible to reach in any other way.

Another serious drawback to the extra long cast is the need for a long, water-disturbing pickup on a strike of a fish or for the recast. The longer the cast, the more fuss you'll make on the water, a point that should be minimized unless you want to put all the fish in the river down for good.

One cure for this, however, is the roll-pickup cast. It is surprising how few even expert fly fishermen retrieve their

lines with this easy and far less disturbing technique. The first time I ever saw it done was while watching my father casting for salmon on the Restigouche in New Brunswick. I was a small boy then and have used this pickup ever since. Watch the next ten good dry-fly anglers on the stream. If one of the ten uses it, he will be the exception.

When you try it you'll be surprised how much easier it is, even though a good deal of slack line has slipped down on the water in front of you. This roll-pickup cast is also the best manner of striking a rising trout, unless of course the cast is short and the direct pullback is then recommended. It is twice as fast as the conventional pullback.

It is easy to perform. Just make believe that you have been roll casting all along and wish to repeat such a cast. Throw a loop of line forward, and as the line begins to lift the leader off the water, pull back hard, even with a double haul. The fly will rise up above its present resting place on the water. At this point pull back hard and quickly false cast. Causing little disturbance on the water, you have control of everything and can get ready to make the next drop down.

Again, the shorter the line, the easier it will be.

Though it has been detailed in most advanced fishing books, the left- or right-hand bend cast is also a must for the angler who would prefer to place the fly over the fish without a devastating amount of leader having to be slashed over his feeding trout.

First time I ever made this cast was with a rod with a terrific set in the tip. Every cast delivered a right-hand loop in the line, and even though I was mad at the rod, I discovered that it placed the fly and not the leader over the fish. I couldn't land a left-hand curve cast with it, but I soon learned how to do it with a rod without a set.

Use that cast almost all the time. You won't get the distance as you would with the straight-out cast, but you'll catch more fish by it.

As I pointed out in *Freshwater Fishing, Tactics on Trout, How To Take Trout,* and other books, these little (or big) subtleties can only be mastered by much need and awareness of the ways to solve stream problems. They take a bit of trial and error, but once mastered, the angler has complete control over his tackle; and it is surprising how much better results he'll have especially when casting over wary and finickey risers.

Most three-year piano students can play all the notes well, but it takes a real pro to put the concert audience into a high.

Performance may be one thing in the demonstration of casting. Certainly a new rod must be put through its paces to see just how well it will perform at all distances, but in the final analysis, when the object of the game is to place that dainty floater in such a position as to fool a trout, the performance may not be as applause gaining as it should, but careful, shorter casts will tip the score in favor of the angler.

And isn't that really what it's all about?

Buy your setup and balance it out for the forty-foot casts, not the sixties, and you'll take trout with the daintiest of all flies, the floater.

Another overdone rod killer and fly destroyer is the habit of over false casting the fly in order to dry it and also to line up the fly for a spot cast. Spider flies quickly become streamers if false cast too fast, too much. Dry flies tend to disintegrate quickly, especially the wings, when false cast too hard, too fast. That zip-zip-zip business may be fun to perform, but for other than the gallery, it is highly unnecessary if the fly is properly dressed and water-proofed.

As I mentioned or implied in the shortest chapter on rods ever written in a book: It makes little difference what rod you use if you don't use it properly. Casts that are too long and line that is unmanageable cannot be cured by spending more money for a better rod.

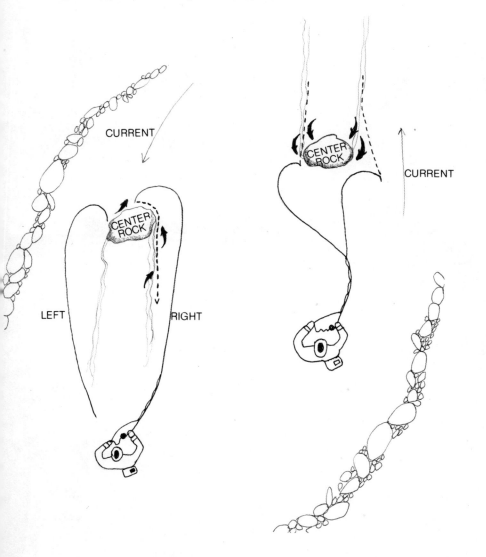

# 9
# Fly Fishing East and West

It is most difficult to write about the famed Beaverkill River in Sullivan County, New York, without writing about the Catskill streams in general, since so many of them originate within shooting distance of each other. These streams all played a large part in the beginnings of traditional trouting in this country, as did similar streams in nearby New Jersey and Pennsylvania.

For nearly forty years I have fished the Beaverkill and its cousins, but before me came the famed anglers of the East and a few experts from foreign lands, namely England and France. On these cherished watercourses I gained much valuable experience learning from such prominent anglers and angler-authors as Edward Hewitt, George LaBranche, Jim Deren, Bill Schaldach, Al Mc-Clane, Larry Koller, and Harry Darbee, to mention only a few. The legendary Theodore Gordon, probably the first man to develop specific fly patterns for the Beaverkill, such as his Quill Gordon, lived out his life on this stream, as did Louis Rhead. Some of my first books were based primarily on these experiences.

Since the Beaverkill is only a few hours from New York, it is a God-given laboratory for authors of fishing books.

Noteworthy is the fact that this stream was the birthplace of bamboo fly-rod development and is rich in the tradition of trout lore in America.

Rocks, gravel, boulders, shelving riffles, deep runs, rapids, still pools, long, slick glides—100 to 200 feet wide in the big river, from 20 to 50 feet wide in the upper river, wadable most of the way, but arm yourself with a wading staff—and watch out for deep holes and swift currents. That's the Beaverkill!

To really get the lay of the land surrounding the Beaverkill, one has to visualize an almost distinct and individual mountain grouping, separate from the Jersey mountains and those of Pennsylvania to the south and west as well as being well below the beginnings of the more northern Adirondack mountains. The Catskill Mountain State Park is situated just west of the Hudson River from Kingston, New York, roughly midway between New York City and Albany, with its southwestern tip reaching over almost to Pennsylvania. Seven principal streams comprise the area's most famous and traditional fishing meccas.

Allow yourself some extra time and take the high mountain road up the east branch of the Neversink from Curry on Route 55, over the "top" and down the north side to Oliveria, the beginning of the south branch of the Esopus. When you reach Route 28 you can go west to the East Branch of the Delaware or east and follow the magnificent Esopus all the way downstream to the Ashokan Reservoir. The Upper Beaverkill is available to view from the car from Livingston Manor up a winding road to Beaverkill, Lewbeach, and Turnwood.

In this region you'll be fishing with anglers of old—the classical anglers who have made it famous not only as the shrine of American angling, particularly American fly fishing, but also one of the best areas of trouting in the east and, in fact, in the Western Hemisphere.

Years ago, in the early days of the Catskills, all of the mountains were covered with a dense and hardy growth of hemlocks, spruces, and pines, with a sprinkling of hardwoods. With the gradual development of the area, the mountainsides were lumbered first for the wood and then for the tannic acid found in tree barks. With more and more cultivation of broad areas of the sloping mountain-

sides added to this, the quality and temperature of the waters gradually changed.

In the days before the brown trout and later the rainbows were imported to these streams, they were teeming with bright, plump, and big brook trout. Anglers from New York would make the two- or sometimes three-day trek from the city in order to angle for them in this untamed wilderness. But then came better roads and the march of civilization, and soon the streams were bordered by railroad beds and road beds, altering the characteristics and conditions of the streams. The last big change for these famed streams has come with the gluttonous need for water from New York City. Reservoirs were plugged into the streams and the roads, once twisting, winding, two-way hardtops, became the present four- and six-lane

highways that will take only a few hours to travel from city desk to stream bank. But still, these streams survive and in some cases are even better fish producers than they were with only the brook trout as the fare.

Because of extreme weather such as hurricanes and high floods, damage takes a high toll; during the past twenty years many of the classical eastern trout streams have almost met their deaths. Strong, flash washouts wreak havoc in the mountains, causing gushing of water down well-carved drainages, widening and in some cases straightening them out into veritable ditches. When these undercut a large section of clay, a landslide can alter the entire course of a stream. This can result in loss of insect hatches, for it takes many years for the new streambed to restore the former ecological balance which had been built up over the years. Damaging effects have just barely been overcome on streams such as Pennsylvania's Brodhead and New York's Catskill streams.

The many ingenious plans for "proper flood control" formulated by the Corps of Engineers are another horror. That these schemes differ from those of Mother Nature doesn't seem to occur to the computers. As a result, the corps has made worse the job that nature started in one of her raw moments.

Despite crises and havoc, nature manages to heal itself, and believe it or not, with the addition of the efforts of local rod and gun clubs, some of the best and most interesting trout fishing is to be had in these famed eastern streams, rivalling anything to be found in many of the touted streams west of the Great Divide. In fact, I've had more interesting times and more times when my accumulated know-how has been stretched to the outer limits on the Beaverkill and especially the Esopus than I've had on the Klamath or Silver Creek. There's something cagey about Catskill streams. I've been busted more times than I care to mention on these waters, and I've seen experts, used to fishing the teeming waters of the West, go down in chagrin as they wade ashore from the 'kill without having felt a rise.

Due to the terrain, the feeder streams are quite remote from road traffic, and much of the mountain area is either too difficult to reach or is owned by private landowners and is heavily posted. Native brook trout are still to be found there. Several clubs, mainly on the Beaverkill, also post much of the upper water. While these restrictions tend to concentrate the fishing activity to the broader and more open lower river sections, they help preserve the fish population and allow unhampered spawning activity. The reservoirs grow big trout that ascend the upper rivers and spawn in the highest mountain tributaries, allowing much natural "wild trout" to form the basis of the fish population which is augmented several times each year by the hatchery trucks. Cold water below the reservoir dams assures much good trout water for many miles.

One word sums up the character of these streams, and that is *rugged*. They are born of an ice-cold spring far up in the heavily wooded and rocky peaks, to carve their twisting way through clay banks and shale and harder rock formations, tumbling all the way until they reach the comparatively rolling gravel and boulder valleys they have carved for themselves. In the fast-moving stretches of the near bottomlands between the sheer cliffs and peaks are pools of quiet water, often and abruptly broken by step-down pools and many fast-water rapids.

## My Esopus

"The Beaverkill has status, but the Esopus has more and bigger fish," is a statement that I made many years ago. I like both rivers for what they are as they are vastly different even though both start high up on the same mountain in the heart of the Catskills. I suppose that it is partly because of Theodore Gordon and subsequent fly-tiers who have fished the Beaverkill because of its distinctive charm and have, because of their words of praise, built up the image of that water to shrine proportions.

Angling history records the names of at least fifty well knowns who sing the praises of that river.

It is surprising how many of these experts could be seen at various times on the Esopus, particularly after the first hatches of Gordons. Hendricksons and March Browns are over then, and the river is very low due to typical summer drought. The Esopus, below the portal at Shandaken, is blessed with a fairly constant flow of water from the through-the-mountains tunnel emptying out from Gilboa

Dam and its source, another Catskill favorite, the Scho-harie River. From the portal down, the river runs at nearly normal height all summer long, thereby creating hatches of big mayflies in the long and deep and fast pools from Mt. Tremper down. Al McClane of *Field & Stream* and his predecessor, Bill Schaldach, could be seen in company with Ray Bergman, Mark Kerridge, Fred Everett, Ted Townsend, Lou Petry, Ray Schrenkeisen, Dan Cahill, Ed Zern, Mel Rosch, Albert Hendrickson, Ray and Dan Holland, Dave Newell, John Tainter Foote, Jim Deren, Don Ray, Art Flick and, today, the modern variety of anglers who are well represented in the realm of angling literature. When they want to get good fishing pictures of sizeable trout, they usually end up on the Esopus. Many pictures of big rainbows that I used in articles in the magazines were taken on the Esopus.

Yet, most pools on this river have never been named as fishing meccas as those of the Beaverkill have been. We just go there to fish and catch big ones, I guess. The Es-opus, like any other river, is tricky, but the odds are with you if you are after trophy trout. Even Larry Koller, a devotee of the lower Neversink, used to go to the Esopus when he wanted enough fish for a big crowd of visitors.

While all of the select streams of this unique corner of the world stem from the same mountainous roots, each has its definite characteristics and devotees. Even those who have preferences fish the others with some constancy. I've been found for days on the upper reaches of the Wil-lowemoc not to catch monster trout, but just because I like this little river. The upper Neversink, well above the big reservoir, is largely private water, and I've poached this and also fished it by invitation. There are stretches of the Beaverkill that are privately owned, and I've fished these and at one time fished the famed waters of the Brooklyn Fly Fishers' Club. But, even with good results and much fun I'd always return to my pet pools and runs of the Esopus. About its only competitor in my book of experi-ence was the lower Neversink, a big broad river edged with gorges and cliffs and twisting deep runs and pools, lots of white water and shelving riffles.

But when I wanted meat I'd fish the Esopus. At times the only way to the best and biggest steaks was by the use of the floating fly.

All these rivers have their source high atop Doubletop and Slide mountains in the lower center of the Catskill State Park. From this high elevation (which is cold country even in summer since its altitude is near the 4,000-foot mark), Roundout Creek flows south through Peekamoose and Bull Run, the east and west branches of the Neversink flow south and a little west to Claryville and down, and the Willowemoc flows southwest to join the Beaverkill at Roscoe. To the north, Dry Brook flows north to join the East Branch of the Delaware at Arkville.

The Esopus has two sources; one comes down directly from Slide Mountain at Winnisook Lodge. It is called the Oliveria until it joins the main stream at Big Indian. The main stream starts above Bushnellsville and flows down to Shandaken where the portal from the Schoharie and Gilboa Dam offer the big river a constant flow all during the summer when other streams including the upper Esopus are way down, exposing the rocks and gravel to a scorching sun.

Most of my fishing has been on the big river from Allaben down to the upper end of the Ashokan Reservoir. Right at the portal there is a big pool close by the road. There are some mighty big brown trout that reside there. They aren't taken on dry flies, though I've seen big noses poking around the surface, which could have been bass, walleyes, or pike. Near Pine Hill are some marvelous series of pools set among some high cliffs, pastoral farmlands, and timbered stretches. But like all of these rivers the lower reaches are usually marked by a railroad on one side and a road on the other. This destroys the pristine glory of a wilderness river, but I must confess I've taken some big trout right in the jagged boulders that were put there years ago by the roadbed builders.

One of the prettiest stretches is the water above and below the junction of Woodland Valley Stream, a small brook that winds its way down a picturesque canyon. Many are the times I've fished this "brook" with tiny dry flies, especially in the early spring, and have taken very big rainbows and a few nice size browns. From here to Phoenicia and the entrance of the Chichester Stream, a medium-sized trout fishery, is one of the best sections of the upper river. The Chichester itself bears need for the selective fly fisherman to work it well all the way to the town of Chichester.

Right at Phoenicia and just below the entrance of the Chichester is the famed and heavily fished Bridge Pool of which I could write a book, since I spent many, many days, weeks, and months in it and the surrounding water during the war years when the only way to get there from New York City was by bus. My fishing then was largely limited to the distance I was willing to walk in my waders, either up or down the river.

The pool immediately below the Bridge Pool, right after a right-angle bend of waterfalls and rushing sluiceway, is Mills Pool, a quarter of a mile long, much of which is over your head. As you might well imagine, it holds some awfully big resident trout and is a major holding pool for the big rainbows that ascend the river from the reservoir every spring and fall when they are on their migratory routes.

From this pool down to Mt. Tremper bridge and pool is fast, broken water that affords fly fishing over fast glides, broken, boulder-strewn water, encompassing a wide expanse of river.

At Mt. Tremper there is again a big drop and long pool, where not only big trout are taken but good-sized smallmouth bass and walleyes. I've seen hatches of big mayflies, and at night, the giant stone flies and action from trout made one think he could only be in the rivers of Montana and Idaho.

Below here, for several miles the river is one succession of big deep pools, broken by fast runs, curved riffs, and deep gorges until it comes to the Five Arch Bridge. Standing on this high spot, you can see for a mile or so upstream and down and look over water that would take a lifetime to really get to know. The Five Arch Bridge pool, just out of sight below, is a haven for those who like their trout big. And they'll take dry flies with abandon only once in a while. If you are lucky to be there at the right hatch and conditions cooperate, you can enjoy dry-fly fishing for trout over the twenty-inch mark that will rival anything you have ever had in the West and only 150 miles from the big city.

This is the water that served as my field for experiments

in fly tying, matching the hatches and discovering some of the mysteries of the current. The limitations of the war years were a blessing in disguise, for I was forced to really work hard at learning trout habits in this stretch of river. It formed the basis of knowledge that could be used under similar situations on other waters around the world some years later.

One might wonder how such a river could contain and supply so many big trout to the host of anglers who fish it year after year. All you have to do is to visit the roadway on the dividing weir of the reservoir some time in late March and see the rainbows and browns jumping the falls to go into the upper reservoir and then to the stream itself. It resembles a salmon run on the great Columbia.

Then consider the tremendous number of excellent feeder streams that offer a natural spawning nursery. Just as an example of its excellence, the stream was stocked with one dumping of rainbow trout back in the thirties, and it has never been repeated. I've seen the times when swarms of little five-inch rainbows along the shallows were so thick you could literally walk on them. This river also affords two spawning seasons for rainbows. Also the browns ascend in the spring as well as the fall, giving us double count on fingerlings. All of the rainbows you hook there are natives and most of the browns over the fifteen-inch mark have either been wild bred or are three-year holdovers. That's hard to beat anywhere in the East.

So, the Esopus has been good to all of us, especially me, in terms of action, and it has also been the stage for some wondrous experiences and the chance meetings of other anglers who have made a marked impression on my life.

## Fly Fishing West

I took the advice of the old saying: "Go West, young man." And I was quite young when I went. From the day I set foot on the train that was to whisk me from Grand Central Station in New York City to the Far West, I have been thankful for the tremendous amount of information that I had gleaned from magazines such as *Field & Stream*. Somehow or other, when I had been reading those magazines back in my home in Connecticut, I had felt that some day the time would come when I'd need all that knowledge of where to fish, how to fish, what tackle to use, and how to fight the big trout the other side of the Great Divide. I was all set in theory, at least. All I needed was the experience. And this I got aplenty.

I've fished for trout and salmon from southern British Columbia, Washington, Oregon, and northern California. I've also worked the dry flies over the best waters of Idaho and Montana with a casual series of short sorties into Colorado, Wyoming, Utah, and Arizona.

Though these visits to famous waters (and some not so famous) were short sometimes, I did manage to gain the flavor of western waters and with Lady Luck's help, managed to creel some nice trout.

One of the biggest revelations has been, I believe, that trout are trout anywhere with slight variations due to their different foods and feeding habits, and what I'd learned by the hard school of taking trout in our over-fished waters of the east has stood me in good stead. On the other hand, I have seen westerners who are quite accomplished at taking lots of big fish from potent western streams become completely skunked and nonplussed by the touchy and selective fifteen-inchers that reside in the Beaverkill or the Battenkill or the Esopus. Many of them, after having savored the rod action provided by Esopus rainbows, have remarked to me that this was some of the best fishing they had ever experienced. They couldn't believe that trout fishing could exist east of St. Louis!

As to my experience with catching those big western trout on flies, my creel has been somewhat limited. I was either on the water too early, too late, the weather was too harsh, water levels too low, or something. Despite all this I can recall many special moments when dry flies did the trick for me, and this served to again put my faith in the dry fly as a practical as well as artful way to feel the action of trout on the rod. More than once I "hunted" successfully for trout with the dry fly when I probably should have been using bucktails or big splotchy-looking nymphs or flappy wet flies. I found that if I were to hunt, the dry fly was the way to go even if no flies were on the water and there was no sign of feeding fish near the surface. There were also times similar to those experienced in the east when during a large fly hatch with the trout busting out all

over, that I failed to have one take a floater of any pattern.

Perhaps you have fished the same waters I have. If so, let's take a quick memory trip to some of them. If you have not, this little excursion might set a pattern for you to follow. In any case, we'll hit some of the high spots.

There's one important advantage of being a member of a club that has affiliates all over the map. The Federation of Fly Fishers of Southern California, numbering several big clubs, has a membership who literally commute from name stream to name stream all over the ten western states. They know what's good and bad about all of the prime waters mainly because they are trying to do something in behalf of the streams and also to perpetuate the sport of fly fishing over wild trout. In their drive to conserve, they get to know these waters intimately.

If it were not for several members of clubs in the Los Angeles area, I'd never have gotten to known about Hot Creek, a very short and inconspicuous bit of trout heaven high in the Sierras. It is the most unusual trout stream in the world, especially the stretch that is owned and controlled by the Hot Creek Ranch. While it might be out of place in this socialist world to mention private water, I must do so, since this parcel of pools serves as the example of what really excellent trout fishing could be like in all of the streams in America. It is perhaps socially improper that this kind of water exists under strictly controlled conditions. But that is where it is at.

The water is located some thirty miles north of Bishop off Highway 395. The creek heads from the mountain passes of the High Sierras and winds its way in a southeasterly direction to the near-desert conditions to be found in the Owens Valley about two miles beyond U.S. Highway 395 to the Hot Creek Springs. From there it flows eastward about ten miles where it joins up with the Owens River.

At the ranch water, the stream is from fifty to a hundred feet wide, medium slow of flow, winding through meadow grass with snowcapped mountains in the background. The temperature of the water is constant due to the hot springs causing it to even out at about fifty-five degrees, a good temperature for the constant and numerous species of insects, particularly mayflies, that live in the water. The grasses and other underwater river foliage argue against the sunken fly; so the dry fly is preferred. The ranch water is controlled by those who enjoy the art of floating flies so no wets or nymphs are used there. Many of the anglers use barbless hooks. It is common practice to be able to hook and release several trout a day that will range from fifteen to thirty inches in length. Some of them have been hooked many times before and have become highly selective.

Another restriction on the water is that no wading is allowed, which in a great respect is responsible for the continued fine growth of weeds and a balanced ecology for the myriads of insect species and thus the fat and fighty trout.

If you ever get to California, don't leave its borders until you have savored the wondrous fishing at Hot Creek. You'll go home a convert to controlled fishing and will extoll the wonders of what trout fishing is there and could be in your hometown stream.

While in California don't neglect the upper Kern or the upper Sacramento and the many tributaries in one of the most scenic parts of the United States, the Mount Shasta country.

The Klamath is a must, if you are to return with stories of big fins and a status that will elevate you to the level of a competent after-dinner speaker.

Up in Oregon is another gem, the Metolius and if you had asked the late Mark Kerridge about his favorite, this one would be it, especially for dry flies. Long, blue-green stretches of moving but not overturbulent rushes, varied bends and eddies with tantalizing deep runs, all framed in by low grassy banks and backed by pine forests. All of it perfect dry-fly water. Here the small flies are the ones that seem to produce, and it took me a long time to discover this fact. One thinks when one fishes western streams and their big waters that big flies would be the medicine. It is just not so, even on the great Deschutes of Oregon and countless others of that state and also in Washington.

While in Oregon mark your road map at the North Umpqua that starts its majestic course from ice pockets and crystal springs deep in the high Cascades at famous Diamond Lake. It then flows steadily downward and to the west for a hundred miles of water that you could never do justice to in a lifetime. These rivers are long and big, full of fish, and they'll fall for the dry fly.

Over in Idaho a top-rated trout stream is Henry's Fork, also known as the North Fork of the Snake, an unbelievable watercourse through this true wilderness state. Box Canyon is top water, especially for dry flies. Some memorable mayfly hatches develop during the latter days of June, through July, and into August. Just south of Last Chance, you'll find top water.

Idaho's Silver Creek, made famous by anglers such as Joe Brooks, hardly needs to be detailed for those who are prone to name dropping of trout waters. It is a haven for experts, and famed outdoor writers and sportsmen from all over the world consider it to be the finest water, particularly dry-fly water, in the Western Hemisphere. While in Idaho, mark down the Upper Salmon and its tributaries the Upper and Middle Forks.

Montana's Big Hole is another top stream that would take a lifetime to get to know well. It is kind to out-of-staters, and the trout seem to aim to please the fly fisherman, if my experience is any measure. I fished the river only once and for two days. Big fish, fighters . . . and unforgettable moments. The Upper Yellowstone should be on the list, and Bud Lilly in West Yellowstone or Dan Bailey in Livingston can set you up. The Flathead, the Boulder, the Firehole, the Gibbons, and the Madison are also musts in the big park.

If one could spend one whole season on these waters, he'd have the equivalent of five lifetimes of prime trout fishing. And that's only a teaser. If you are in the mood to try this high country, I suggest you read, for more specific coverage of the ten states, my friend Duncan Campbell's book *88 Trout Streams of the West,* published by Western Outdoors Magazine, Costa Mesa, California.

Someday, books will be written about each of these fine rivers and in them records of the time, energy, talent, and fight that sportsmen and conservationists have spent in not only trying to preserve but to improve these waters. It is a heritage that all of us, even if we never get to fish them, should fight for through membership in organizations such as Trout Unlimited and the Federation of Fly Fishermen.

# 9
# Crystal Balling It
# to the Exit

The middle seventies saw the world do a turnaround. The greatest threats to mankind, pollution, starvation, and overpopulation had forced nations into a vortex of seething crises. Gross National Product—a slogan of the spiraling accumulation of goods—more inflation, greater materialistic demands doubled back on themselves, and people began to rearrange their thinking and to develop new reasons for being. The ecological picture changed almost overnight. The frightful cycle of two centuries was reversed and man, finding that seven-lane highways led nowhere, decided to stop, not stop progress or evolution, but to reconsider what was important.

The dilemma was a tough one to handle, and for some time the leaders and the led were in confusion, somewhat like ants when someone steps on the ant hill. But, like ants, they regrouped and survived. Science that had been leading mankind down the road to ruin, suddenly came up with life-saving answers. Sincere ecologists whose warnings had long fallen on deaf ears were now running things.

Outdoor recreation became a way of life fifty-two weeks out of the year, not just two weeks. Man had decided that two out of fifty-two was a lousy return on his money.

By 1980, firm stands as to the uses of all natural resources had come under the management of a team of specialists in living, no longer being exploited for mere production and consumption.

The Federation of Fly Fishers, a small group of dedicated sportsmen formed way back in the 1960's, now had a million members, all conservationists. The Izaak Walton League had a strong voice in Congress. Trout Unlimited had become a federal bureau.

The trout had been made a special game fish, a status which elevated them to a restricted sphere in the sporting scene. Hunting and fishing were national sports as popular as baseball and every blade of grass, every tree, every park, every bit of open land reflected the new lifestyle.

Fishing tackle developed to unbelievable heights. Material for fly making had been completely revolutionized. Trout fishing was a recreation of the highest order, as was the sport of catching other game fish.

A significant outcome was that people were returned to the soil. No longer were they caged in cities and close

quarters like chickens that never see the ground (much less walked on it). This return to the earth elements gave people a balance to their reason for living and respect for the earth.

Fly fishing was still fly fishing. It hadn't changed much in its psychology, reason for being, and art. In fact it expanded beyond the dreams of the most fervent of those old anglers living back in 1977.

In reflecting over the years since then, a recent correspondent wrote in a world fishing magazine (dated 1985) that all of the hundred million fly fishermen should bow down to their predecessors who had foreseen what was coming. They had smelled and sneezed at pollution long before the general population had. They had warned, but nobody had listened.

Then finally the word had struck home: *death*. This word was rejected and the word *live* was substituted. It was quite a revolution. The Royal Coachman was adopted as a national symbol and all was well.

A statement by the ancient sage, Juvenal, became the working slogan of the world: "Never does Nature say one thing and wisdom another."

We can add that information and computers do not produce wisdom. *That* comes from somewhere else!

## Exit Casting

Many pages of rough typing are behind me and now I can sit back at last and read what others have been writing about my sport over the years. I've stayed away from them, not for fear of influence, but because I've wanted to write about fishing as I see it, especially the dry-fly fishing aspect.

My main objective in writing books is to offer something for the beginner, especially. I've left the expert, post-graduate writing to such as Ernie Schwiebert and Charlie Fox and the rest. I figure that if I can get the beginner started, he'll develop into an expert sooner or later and with this development will also evolve into a true conservationist. We need many of these, and the quickest way they come into being is when fishermen see their fishing going to pot. No matter what the causes.

I'm also going to do a lot more fishing. As a matter of fact, I've a fly rod all rigged up and it is standing in the corner. Near where I live in Ormond Beach, Florida, is a small creek that empties into the Intracoastal Waterway. There are school tarpon there that jump like salmon. Chances are that they will not take dry flies, but I'm confident that they will take some of my specially designed streamers. Then, again, I just *might* try a Royal Coachman over them. One can never tell about fisherman's luck, especially when using a fly with such a broad and excellent record.

So, I exit casting . . . and with the hope that you will fish a bit harder and longer and better and with more enjoyment of your hours astream and with more fish to your credit whether you creel them or set them loose to fight again another day.

Just remember, those of us who write to and for you are not really gods just because we are in print. It still remains that you read all you can and then put the books down and exit casting.

# Index

# A

Across-and-downstream drift
    cast, 91
Adirondack Mountains, 79
Allagash River, 3, 74, 124
Angler's Roost, 25
Ants, 59–60
Arizona, 157
Ashokan Reservoir, 154
Atherton, John, 25–26
Atlantic salmon, 41
Ausable River, 74, 77, 79

# B

Bailey, Dan, 163
Bates, Jo, 95
Battenkill River, 157
Beaverkill River, 45, 71, 77,

137, 154, 157
    fly fishing on, 145–151
Bergman, Ray, 134, 152
Big Hole River, 163
Black Bucktail, 97
Black Dose, 25
Black Marabou, 97
Black Quill, 90, 94
Blackfly, 16
Black-and-White Marabou,
    97
Blue Quill, 68, 90, 94
Boot foot waders, 116
Boulder River, 163
Box Canyon, 162
Bridge Pool, 155
British Columbia, 3, 157
Brooklyn Fly Fishers' Club,
    152
Brooks, Joe, 134, 163
Brown Bucktail, 97
Brown Bucktail-Streamer, 98
Brown Drake, 87

## Z